GREAT SPORTING FAILURES

GREAT SPORTING FAILURES

GEOFF TIBBALLS

CollinsWillow
An Imprint of HarperCollins*Publishers*

First published in 1993 by
Collins Willow
an imprint of HarperCollins*Publishers*
London

© Geoff Tibballs 1993

A CIP catalogue record for this book
is available from the British Library

ISBN 0 00 218526 1

Illustrations by Richard G. Jolley

Printed and bound in Great Britain by
Cox & Wyman Ltd

CONTENTS

INTRODUCTION

I remember the moment well. It was the first time at school that we had been told to do the hop, step and jump (an event known in more enlightened circles as the triple jump). I stood on the runway, a coiled spring waiting to explode into action and a few other mixed metaphors besides. I sprinted as fast as I could, hopped like Skippy the bush kangaroo, stepped for all I was worth and jumped higher than any salmon. I came to earth with a resounding thud, my throbbing ankle telling me that I had definitely not landed in sand. As I looked around, the reason was plain to see – I was still on the runway, four or five feet from the pit. There and then I abandoned what hopes I had of becoming the next Fred Allsop. It was another sport to add to my list of 'can't do'.

My first inkling that I was not destined for great things in the world of sport came with the awful realization that mine always seemed to be the last name called out when we picked up teams before football. I was even behind the class fatty. When I did attempt to prove my critics wrong and show my mettle as a goalkeeper, I was hindered by a full-back who insisted on telling me jokes, the punch-line invariably arriving just as the ball disappeared into the back of my net.

There were, of course, occasions when I threatened to rise above the abysmal. One lunchtime on Camber Sands, I thought I had mastered the art of off-break bowling when producing a delivery that pitched and turned to take off-stump – well, the edge of the picnic box. It was only when lying on the same stretch of beach some hours later that I realized the 'turn' may have had something to do with the fact that the beach sloped down to the sea at that point.

Then there was the time when, in a moment of recklessness, the school picked me for the cross-country team, an activity considered only marginally more offensive than being chosen for the school choir. I trailed in 15th out of 16 and would probably have fared even worse had the boy I finished ahead of not been reduced to a virtual cripple after impaling his foot on a metal spike. As it was, he nearly caught me on the run-in.

I thought that perhaps like a fine wine I might improve with age but an unorthodox golf swing which sent many a drive on to my left foot made me realize that I was really just a cheap table plonk. My final humiliation came two years ago in the fathers' race at school sports day when, dazzled by the competing array of shell suits, I came in a dismal last at the running-with-the-ball-between-your-knees race. Indeed I would still be out there now had I not picked the blessed ball up and walked the last 50 yards. My protests that it was not an officially recognized Olympic sport and how would Seb Coe have been expected to run under such a ridiculous handicap, fell on deaf ears.

People who were there that fateful afternoon still point at me in the street. My daughter hasn't spoken to me since. With that, I decided to hang up my boots, rackets and clubs and concentrate on something less energetic such as Junior Scrabble. This book is dedicated to all those who have suffered similar experiences. It is living proof that we are not alone.

Geoff Tibballs
May 1993

SOCCER

BACK FROM THE DEAD

Surely the least successful tribute in the history of soccer was that organized by HFS Loans League team Congleton. Players and spectators were forced to call off a minute's silence to mourn the death of the club's oldest fan...when he turned up at the ground. Die-hard supporter Fred Cope, aged 85, set off as usual on 27 February 1993 to watch the Cheshire club's fixture with Rossendale. Arriving at the ground, he saw the club's flag flying at half-mast but assumed it was in tribute to former England captain Bobby Moore who had died that week. But when Fred began to read the match-day programme, he was horrified to see it contained his own obituary, complete with a photograph. So as the players and the referee lined up on the pitch to pay their last respects, Fred thought he had better point out to officials that rumours of his death were greatly exaggerated. The confusion arose after another fan had innocently spread a rumour that Fred had died. Congleton manager Bill Wright said: 'We took him at his word and thought it would be nice to give Fred a tribute as he is so popular.' In a supreme understatement, he added: 'It was a shock when Fred turned up.' To underline his well-being, Fred went on to win a bottle of whisky in the half-time raffle.

TOOTH FAIRY

A tense finish to a Danish league match in April 1960 saw Norager hanging on to a 4–3 lead against Ebeltoft with just seconds remaining. Referee Henning Erikstrup was on the point of blowing the final whistle when suddenly his dentures fell out. As he ignominiously scrambled around on

the pitch in an effort to recover them, Ebeltoft equalized. Despite vehement and somewhat understandable protests from Ebeltoft, Mr. Erikstrup disallowed the goal, replaced his false teeth and promptly blew for full-time.

BASKET CASE

When the famous Harlem Globetrotters came to London in the early 1960s, among those who went to watch their unique form of basketball wizardry was Fulham goalkeeper Tony Macedo. Sadly Macedo decided to imitate their antics

in Fulham's next match, against Spurs at Craven Cottage.
Collecting the ball, he bounced it with either hand as he ran
round the penalty-area, these being the days before the four-
step law for goalkeepers. For an encore, he mimicked the
clowning style of Meadowlark Lemon, pretending that he
was going to throw the ball to an opponent. But just as
Macedo switched his aim to team-mate Johnny Haynes, the
ball slipped out of his grasp straight to the feet of the
unmarked Jimmy Greaves. Macedo was left to reflect on his
folly as he picked the ball out of the net.

THE LINESMAN SAW RED

We all know that linesmen not only have excellent
eyesight and two parents but are completely
unbiased. However some doubts do have to be
expressed about the behaviour of a flag-bearer in a
minor Italian league game between Tresana and Santa
Anastasia. The linesman in question was an official
with Tresana, a situation not guaranteed to ensure
impartiality, and took exception when the referee
awarded a free-kick against his club. He immediately
raced on to the pitch wielding his flag and set about the
entire Santa Anastasia team. In a performance of which
Sylvester Stallone would have been proud, he left one
player with a broken nose, another with a black eye
and a third with a badly bruised face.

THANKS, REF

A Barrow shot sailing harmlessly wide struck referee Ivan
Robinson and deflected into the net for the only goal of the
1968 clash with visiting Plymouth. As one Plymouth player
remarked: 'It was a long way to go to be beaten by a goal from
the ref.'

UNITED FANS SAW BLUE

Student Julian Fiddler sat down to watch his 21st birthday present, the video *Manchester United – Hall Of Fame*, but instead he and a mate found themselves engrossed in an American blue movie called Satin Angels. They wondered why the players started swapping shirts in the first minute. Julian said: 'We were expecting to see George Best and Bobby Charlton but we got this film of women making love to each other and couples having sex all over the place. A friend and I bought it from the Virgin store in Leeds – but there certainly weren't any virgins in the film.' Two girl students who shared the house walked out in disgust but Julian and his pal kept going well into extra-time. Virgin, who on learning of the mix-up sent Julian a genuine copy of the United film, said that the wrong label had been put on the video while it was being duplicated. All copies were removed from the shelves for checks. It was a horrible job, but somebody had to do it.

THE STRIFE OF BRIAN

Exeter City manager Brian Godfrey was so appalled with the all-round ineptitude displayed by his team during a 5–1 defeat at Millwall one Sunday in 1982 that as punishment he kept his players in London overnight to play Millwall's reserves the next day. Godfrey could only look on in anguish as Exeter even managed to lose to the Lions' second string 1–0.

BAPTISM OF FIRE

Keeping goal for Halifax Town has always been a full-time occupation, but never more so than for Steve Milton who marked his debut by letting in 13 at Stockport in Division Three North on 6 January 1934. Town lost 13–0.

STERLING CRISIS

The remarkable managerial skills of the Sterling family undoubtedly played a major part in the achievements of South London boys' team Coleridge Rovers in 1992–93. With Sally Sterling at the helm and husband Fred as club chairman, the team of 11 to 13-year-olds succeeded in losing their first dozen games, conceding no fewer than 200 goals in the process. But eventually a 35–0 thrashing was too much for Fred to take and, displaying commendable ruthlessness, he sacked his wife. Fred realized there was really only one man for the job – himself. So he took over as manager and waited for the improvement. It soon came – Coleridge only lost their next match 30–0! Fred explained: 'I had to fire Sally. It wasn't her fault – she simply couldn't handle how bad we were.'

WRIGHT IDIOT

We hear many tales of goalscorers being in a rich vein where they hit the back of the net with almost monotonous regularity. The same applied to Everton defender Tommy Wright in the spring of 1972. Over a period of four days this previously unsung hero scored twice – but both were own goals. Nor did Wright choose just any old matches in which to make his mark on the scoresheet. He began on 4 March with a first-minute own goal in the fiercely-contested Merseyside derby with Liverpool at Anfield. Within a week, again selecting the opening 60 seconds as the perfect time to surprise his own goalkeeper, Wright struck once more, this time to the benefit of Manchester United at Old Trafford. Sadly, after that his career went into decline and he returned to being a perfectly competent defender.

STANDING ROOM ONLY

M embers of the Falkirk sporting fraternity who thought
they had better set off early for the vital Scottish Second
Division basement battle between East Stirlingshire and
Leith on 15 April 1939 need not have bothered. For only 32
spectators turned up – the lowest attendance for a senior
league game in Britain. There were no reports of any crowd
disturbances.

TAKING IT TO HEARTS

M ost club directors are renowned for their generosity
in defeat as they dispense Scotch and bonhomie in
the boardroom after the match. Alas, Hearts director
Douglas Park (no relation to Hamilton Academicals'
ground) allowed his feelings to get the better of him
following a hard-fought home clash with Rangers in
1988. Indeed he was so infuriated by David Symes'
refereeing that he locked the match official in his
changing-room for 18 minutes after the game and
marched off with the key. Not altogether surprisingly,
the Scottish League took a dim view of this unsporting
behaviour and fined Park £1,000. He also resigned as a
Hearts director.

SWIFT ACTION

A ngered by the verbal derision which greeted his arrival for
the match with Goldenhill Boys' Club in 1975, Glasgow
referee Mr Tarbet booked all 11 Glencraig United players
plus both substitutes in their dressing-room before a ball had
been kicked.

SHORT-LIVED COMEBACK

*S*tephen Gould made the mistake of not suffering in silence as he watched his works team from Little Aston in Staffordshire lose week after week. Instead he persisted in criticizing the goalkeeper to the extent that he was finally challenged to show whether he could do any better. Gould had been a goalkeeper at school and so at the age of 40, inspired by golden oldies such as Peter Shilton and Pat Jennings, he agreed to make a less-than-eagerly-awaited comeback. 'Wearing one of the new multi-coloured jerseys and giant Sepp Maier gloves, I really felt the part as I ran out for the pre-match warm-up. I did some gymnastic exercises on the goal-line to loosen up and then jumped up and touched the crossbar.' This was his second fatal mistake for as he did so, the bar came crashing down on to his head and he was carried back to the dressing-room. He lamented: 'My comeback was over without a shot being fired.'

UNHAPPY CHRISTMAS

It takes a certain lack of discipline to be sent off after just 20 seconds, but to perform the feat on Christmas Day raises the perpetrator to the highest echelons of ineptitude. Thus Wrexham's Ambrose Brown enters the hall of fame following his swift dismissal by referee Bert Mee in the Division Three North encounter with Hull City on 25 December 1936. His one consolation could have been that he was first home for Christmas lunch.

UNWANTED AWARD

His own goal having secured promotion for Nottingham Forest in 1977, grateful Forest supporters voted Millwall's Jon Moore their Player of the Year that evening.

MISPLACED CONFIDENCE

Preston North End were one of the country's most powerful teams in soccer's formative years and accordingly they definitely fancied their chances of defeating West Bromwich Albion in the 1888 FA Cup Final. So confident were Preston that they asked to be photographed with the Cup before the game, pointing out that they were liable to be dirty afterwards and a lack of cleanliness might mar the picture. The match referee, a Major Marindin, politely inquired: 'Had you not better win it first?' Wise words, for too proud Preston lost 2–1 in what was described at the time as the greatest upset in the Cup's short history.

KEEPER FOULED BY FORD SIERRA

Bernie Marsh, the goalkeeper with Mid Sussex League strugglers Balcombe Reserves, had already earned a reputation for eccentricity by letting in 100 goals for the bottom-of-the-table outfit in the 1992–93 season. But he

*surpassed himself in a match at Hartfield by managing to
collide with a Ford Sierra in his own goalmouth. In fairness
to the hapless custodian, it wasn't exactly his fault. After all,
how many goalkeepers expect to encounter a car being
driven along the six-yard line while a match is in progress? It
happened five minutes from time with the game delicately
poised at 1–1. As play moved to the half-way line, spectator
Tony Nana decided it was safe to back his car on to the
pitch to turn round since his exit was blocked by other
vehicles. Alas his manoeuvre coincided with a high lob
being hoisted towards the Balcombe goal. As Bernie raced
back, he was blissfully unaware of what was happening
behind him and crashed his head into the side of the car,
knocking himself out. Recovering from his ordeal, he
reflected: 'The ball went up high and all I could hear was my
mates shouting at me. I thought they were egging me on to
save the shot and I was really determined not to let another
goal in. But they must have been warning me about the car.
I touched the ball over the bar and the next thing I was out
cold.' The match was abandoned and from now on Bernie
will be ultra-cautious in case future opponents send the
Dormobile up for corners.*

SCOTTISH SAGA

The least successful attempt to stage a football match must
surely be that of Inverness Thistle whose second round
Scottish Cup tie with Falkirk was postponed a record 29
times due to bad weather. It was eventually played on 22
February 1979, 47 days after the original date. When the
beleaguered Inverness groundstaff finally got the pitch ready
for play, they must have wondered whether it was worth all
the effort as Falkirk triumphed 4–0. Not that Falkirk's joy
lasted too long either – three days later they were knocked
out of the Cup 3–0 by Dundee!

FLAG DAY

In a local league match at Bedford, referee Fred Seaton once sent off an entire team of Italian immigrants for wading into 300 spectators when somebody snatched their linesman's flag.

FLATTERED TO DECEIVE

Courage Colts were quietly confident when they took an early lead against Midas FC in an under-14 League fixture in Kent on 11 April 1976, only for Midas to strike back and run out the somewhat comprehensive 59–1 winners. And it was only a 70-minute game. The after-match inquest suggested that maybe Courage were wrong to try and sit back on their lead.

GARY'S GOOF

In the annals of goalkeeping history, the name of Leeds United's Gary Sprake is synonymous with classic displays liberally interspersed with moments of supreme incompetence. His finest hour was at Anfield in December 1967 when he succeeded in throwing the ball into his own net. Reliving the anguish, Sprake said: 'I was going to throw the ball wide to Terry Cooper when he screamed "No, no" because Ian Callaghan was closing him down. So I went to pull the ball back to my chest, as I often did, and it just flew over my left shoulder into the net. There was silence for a minute. I didn't know what to do. Jack Charlton had his back to me and was talking to the ref who then gave a goal. It happened a minute before half-time and as we were walking off, the disc jockey announced "This record is dedicated to Gary Sprake" and put on *Careless Hands* by Des O'Connor. Sprake remains philosophical about his mishap. 'The manager Don Revie never said anything, the lads said I was unlucky and I provided Big Jack with one of his better after-dinner stories...'

CORRIGAN'S CLANGER

*O*n his day, Manchester City goalkeeper Joe Corrigan was
*nearly in the same class as Gary Sprake. Corrigan peaked
in a match with West Ham when, drop-kicking from the
right-hand side of his penalty area, he screwed the ball
across the pitch straight to West Ham's Ronnie Boyce,
standing some 40 yards from goal. Boyce promptly volleyed
it back into the empty net as a bemused Corrigan looked on.*

SHEEP DIP

Possibly the unluckiest mascot in the history of soccer
was Toby the sheep who was supposed to bring good
fortune to Scottish club Greenock Morton in the years
leading up to the First World War. Sadly, after one
match while the team celebrated their victory in a local
hostelry, Toby was left in the changing-room and
drowned in the players' bath.

SETTING THE RIGHT EXAMPLE

Sensing that an under-13s match at Ascot in Berkshire was
too one-sided to be interesting, the players' parents livened
matters up by starting a touchline brawl which resulted in
the police being called to separate the warring factions and
the game being abandoned. Theale Tigers were leading arch
rivals Great Holland Dynamos 6–0 when a linesman
allegedly clipped one of the players around the ear following a
bad tackle. A spectator said: 'One of the dads running the line
appeared to clip a lad. Another father ran up and had to be
restrained. Then everybody piled in. It was pandemonium.'
Tigers' secretary Jim Brown observed: 'All the boys behaved
impeccably – unlike their parents.'

TRAINER CARRIED OFF

*T*he inaugural World Cup in 1930 was notable for a fine
performance from the trainer of the United States team
during their semi-final with Argentina. Still incensed by a
controversial Argentinian goal, the US medic ran on to the
pitch to tend an injured player, yelling abuse at the referee
as he did so. In a fit if pique, he threw down his medical bag,
broke a bottle of chloroform and accidentally anaesthetized
himself. His ignominy was complete when he had to be
carried off by his own team. Not noted for their sense of
humour, the Argentinians refused to enter into the spirit of
things and went on to win 6–1.

CHAIRMAN SENT OFF

As a result of an injury crisis, 37-year-old David
Lane, chairman of Vauxhall Leaguers Tring Town,
was named as a substitute for their local derby with
Berkhamsted in season 1990–91. His moment of
glory finally arrived when he was summoned from
the bench to join the action, only to be sent off
before he had even kicked the ball!

PRINCE OF WAILS

No Welsh club has ever been Football League Champions – a
state of affairs that is solely down to the efforts of one
man, Cardiff City's Len Davies. In the last minute of the last
match of the 1923–24 season, Cardiff were drawing 0–0 at
Birmingham when they were awarded a penalty. All the
Welshmen needed to do was score and they would pip
Huddersfield for the First Division title. Naturally in view of
the significance of the kick, there was no rush of volunteers

to take it. Eventually Len Davies strode forward, placed the ball on the spot and missed. Cardiff lost out on the Championship on goal average.

IN THE SACK

*I*n 1992 the trainer of a German club was fired for falling in love with the centre-forward. Forty-six-year-old Roland Eybe, a coach from Delmenhorst, became infatuated with Anja Bresch, 23, the star striker with the women's team. He got the boot after his wife walked out and half of the players quit because he spent so little time trying to improve the side's miserable record.

WORLD-CLASS LOSERS

Bulgaria have the worst record of any country in the final stages of the World Cup. They have played 16 matches – and haven't won one. But they are certainly pretty adept at thinking up excuses as to why they got beaten. Following a 1993 World Cup qualifier defeat at the hands of Austria, Bulgarian manager Dimitar Penev produced a splendid exoneration. 'We were the victims of Austrian dirty tricks before the game started,' he claimed with more than a hint of indignation. 'First they hoisted a flag which was nothing like the Bulgarian one. Then the band played a dreadful version of our anthem. My players are a patriotic bunch and were very angry. The team's composure and concentration disappeared and that's why we lost.' Clearly Mr. Penev's guidelines could be of great benefit to our own managers. It's just a shame Doncaster hasn't got a national anthem.

THE CROWD WAS UNSIGHTED

There was huge expectancy as the Crystal Palace staged its first FA Cup Final in 1895. A crowd of 42,000, at the time a record for a game in London, turned up to see Aston Villa play West Bromwich Albion. But because of mass confusion at the turnstiles, what most of them didn't see was the game's only goal, scored within 30 seconds of the kick-off when a shot from Villa's Bob Chatt was deflected past the West Brom keeper. Thus Villa fans watched the remaining 89 minutes deprived of their moment of glory while West Brom supporters probably didn't even know their side was losing.

HELPING HAND

That old footballing adage about always playing to the whistle once rebounded on Chelsea defender John Sillett in a match against Sheffield Wednesday. Thinking the referee had blown for an infringement, Sillett caught the ball in his own penalty area but the whistle he had heard had not come from the match official but from a spectator. As the referee awarded the inevitable penalty, Sillett confessed: 'I felt the size of a pin-head.'

GOAL FAMINE

In early 1993 Third Division Hartlepool, bored with mid-table anonymity, gallantly set about shattering the endurance record for the longest spell without a goal. Following Andy Saville's last-minute penalty in the 1–0 FA Cup giant-killing defeat of Crystal Palace, they contrived to go over 13 matches without hitting the back of the net. The total stood at an impressive 1221 minutes when on 6 March at Blackpool, that man Saville had the misfortune to score the equalizer in a 1–1 draw. His punishment was immediate: a transfer to Birmingham City.

PAID THE PENALTY

Siminiota, a defender with Brazilian club San Lorenzo, thought he had a 2–1 victory bonus over Estudiantes in the bag when he picked up the ball in injury time believing that it had gone out of play. So he was stunned when referee Humberto Dellacasa, who had already given two hotly-disputed penalties, ruled that it hadn't – and awarded Estudiantes a spot-kick. The penalty was converted and in the resulting furore, two players were sent off for manhandling the referee who had to be escorted from the pitch by baton-wielding riot police. Really, just an ordinary game in South America.

SPOT THE BALLS-UP

The prize for the least successful attempt to organize a spot-the-ball competition goes to the Cardiff-based *Western Mail* who in January 1993 mistakenly printed the previous week's solution instead of the current poser. As a result, instead of the ball being blanked out, it loomed large in the sky. And in case readers couldn't believe their eyes, a huge white arrow pin-pointed its precise location. The contest really did live up to its slogan: 'It's so easy to be a winner.' The own-goal was spotted after 1,000 copies of the paper had been run off the presses and all but a handful were frantically withdrawn. The *Mail's* technical director admitted ruefully: 'It would have been no problem for anyone to spot that ball. I've now got a skip full of papers with the world's easiest spot-the-ball competition.'

COMYN ON STRONG

Few substitutes have made a more immediate impact than Derby's Andy Comyn, brought on in the 78th minute of the game with Bristol City at the Baseball Ground on 6 September 1992. He came on as City were awarded a free-kick near the half-way line. The ball was floated into the penalty area where Comyn rose high to head his first touch firmly into his own net past stand-in keeper Paul Williams. It was estimated that he had been on the field less than 10 seconds when he made his decisive intervention. Inspired by such benevolence, City went on to win 4–3.

LAW BREAKER

Sidelined through injury, Denis Law was forced to view Manchester United's 1968 European Cup semi-final with Real Madrid from the bench. Forgetting himself for a

moment, Law was so excited when Bill Foulkes scored that he punched the air in his familiar style, only for his fist to smash through the roof of the dug-out. Nursing a broken bone, Law remarked: 'Marvellous. I even get injured watching the game.'

KILLIE CRANKY

When Kilmarnock bravely entered the inaugural Scottish FA Cup in 1873, they overlooked one minor point – they were more accustomed to playing rugby than soccer. Consequently their tie with Renton in October of that year developed into something of a farce. The *Glasgow Evening News* reported that the Kilmarnock team was not 'thoroughly conversant with Association rules. On account of this, the Renton club kept the ball well up to the goal posts of their opponents as they received several free-kicks in succession thro' some of the Auld Killie's men persistently using their hands.' In the circumstances it was not altogether surprising that Kilmarnock lost 3–0.

FALSE HOPE

Few clubs have shown more commendable optimism than Fulham who, despite losing 10–0 to Liverpool at Anfield in the first leg of their League Cup tie in 1986, printed details in their programme of what would happen should the tie be all-square at the end of 90 minutes' play in the second leg. Sadly, the players failed to take the hint and Liverpool won 3–2 for an aggregate victory of 13–2.

PRAYERS WEREN'T ANSWERED

A pre-match ritual for Isadore Irandir, goalkeeper with Brazilian team Rio Preto, was to say his prayers in the goalmouth. He adopted his customary pose as Corinthians kicked off in a match at the Bahia Stadium. But he had reckoned without the renowned left foot of Roberto Rivelino who, accepting the ball straight from the kick off, blasted a shot from the half-way line. It sailed into the back of the Rio Preto net after just three seconds' play, en route whistling past the ear of a startled Senhor Irandir who was still on his knees concluding his beseechments to the Almighty.

THE REFEREE SCORED

Instructions to referees go along the lines of ensuring that the rules of the game are obeyed and keeping the score. They do not under any circumstances invite the match official to attempt to demonstrate to the players that he is a better footballer than they are. But losing control of a Sunday League fixture in Southampton, the referee became so frustrated that he decided to show off his skills instead. The game was between a local gasworks side and their bitter rivals from the electricity company. Sparks flew and the referee was taking more names than an autograph hunter. At half-time he warned the players that if they did not cut out the rough stuff, he would abandon the match. One of the gasworks players takes up the story: 'Midway through the second-half I exchanged passes with a team-mate on the edge of the penalty area when suddenly the referee pounced in between us and fired an unstoppable shot into the top corner of the net. "That," he said, "is how you're supposed to play the game." Then he tossed his whistle to a linesman and walked off the pitch, never to be seen again.' Stunned by this inspired interruption, the players allowed the game to drift to a peaceful and uneventful conclusion.

HUNG OVER

As the 1908–9 season drew to a close, Leicester Fosse, already doomed to relegation from the First Division, had one thing to look forward to – the wedding of a team-mate. So they went out and celebrated his nuptials in style, the day before facing Nottingham Forest in a match crucial to Forest's safety. Fosse crashed 12–0 and the two points ensured that Forest stayed in the top flight. Suspicious of what was then a record score for Division One and between near neighbours, a Football League Commission launched an inquiry into the circumstances surrounding the match. But far from uncovering any hint of foul play or bribery, the Commission concluded that Fosse's miserable performance was solely down to the fact that they were still hung over from the wedding.

CONSOLATION PRIZE

Barton Athletic, beaten in all 26 matches in the Darlington and District League, were surprised to find that at the end of their dismal 1992–93 season, their efforts had been recognized with a trophy. They had won the League's fair-play award. A club official said: 'We've always been a very popular club – particularly with our opponents.'

A WISE SWITCH

As a young schoolboy in Bolton, future England centre-forward Nat Lofthouse's first game was in goal. His team lost 7–1.

NERVOUS WRECKS

*S*eized with a sudden spirit of adventure, Scottish club Raith Rovers decided to embark on an overseas tour to the Canary Islands in 1930. But on the way their vessel capsized and they were shipwrecked. Happily, all players and officials were rescued but thereafter Raith tended to settle for friendlies closer to home amid the less tropical climes of Cowdenbeath and Dunfermline.

WRONG TWIN SENT OFF

*W*hen Paul Pullen, a player with Diadora League outfit Bognor, became involved in a skirmish with opponents Dulwich Hamlet, the referee inadvertantly sent off his identical twin brother Mick instead. Mick, Bognor's player-manager, protested his innocence but the referee would have none of it. 'The ref called me over and gave me my marching orders,' said Mick. 'I told him it wasn't me. Paul thought it was hilarious but I'll make sure he serves the three-match suspension!'

THE PLOT SICKENS

*I*t appears that some clubs will go to any lengths to avoid relegation but few plans have been so hopelessly ill-conceived as that of a French team from Sully-sur-Loire near Orleans. Their masterstroke was to lace the visiting side's lemonade with knock-out drops. Even the most naive referee must have suspected something when players started collapsing all around him. Thus the offending club's treachery was uncovered and they were reported to the authorities. Their punishment? Relegation.

REFEREES IN BRAWL

A game between two teams of referees in Spain should have
been just about the best-behaved fixture on the calendar.
But it ended in uproar after the match official sent one off
and was promptly felled by a blow from the disgraced
player's father, also a referee.

MORROW SORROW

R arely has a post-match celebration gone more awry than
that following Arsenal's 1993 Coca Cola Cup final victory
over Sheffield Wednesday. As the Gunners' skipper Tony
Adams hoisted young match-winner Steve Morrow on high,
he lost his balance and Morrow crashed to the ground,
breaking his upper right arm. So while his team-mates went
up to collect the Cup, Morrow was stretchered off to the
dressing-room, his face covered by an oxygen mask. His
injury meant he missed the FA Cup final.

SALAD DRESSING

B eleaguered Chelsea keeper Dave Beasant spent the first weeks of the 1993–4 season with his right foot in plaster after dropping a jar of salad cream on his big toe, thereby severing the tendon. 'I couldn't believe it,' groaned Beasant. 'I tried to catch the falling jar with my foot. Everyone thought it was funny but it couldn't have come at a worse time for me. And the jar smashed on the floor anyway!'

SNATCH OF THE DAY

C ardiff City were jubilant after taking record receipts of over £50,000 from their FA Cup tie with Queen's Park Rangers on 6 January 1990. They were less ecstatic when they later discovered that thieves had escaped with most of the money.

HIS LORDSHIP ENTERTAINS

W hen Millwall moved from the Isle of Dogs to The Den on 22 October 1910, the opening ceremony was to be conducted by the distinguished Lord Kinnaird, President of the FA, before the match with Brighton. Unfortunately, while the other guests and club officials were waiting at the Cold Blow Lane end of the ground, Lord Kinnaird had inadvertantly gone to the opposite end. With proceedings ready to start, his Lordship had to be unceremoniously hauled, pushed and pulled over the wall into the ground. He then had to dash the length of the pitch without tripping over his beard. All in all, it was scarcely the most dignified of entrances.

FOOD FOR THOUGHT

A Spanish newspaper reported that a group of neo-Nazi fans had been trying to extort money from Real Madrid players in exchange for their support. This interesting precedent came to light after the Ultra Sur, who take their name from the end of the Real stadium where members hang their neo-Nazi banners, allegedly demanded 'tips' from midfielder Rafael Martin Vazquez. When Vazquez rejected their demands, it is said that gang members waited outside the locker room to 'give him a scare'. The Ultra Sur also spat at Real keeper Pedro Jaro following a UEFA Cup defeat at Paris St. Germain but these hardened thugs were persuaded to stop when an official bought them off with a plate of left-over sandwiches. Imagine the Krays being convinced to mend their ways on a promise of half a dozen sausage rolls and a tray of vol-au-vents...

POINTLESS PROTEST

A fter losing 3–1 to Darwen in the first round of the FA Cup in 1890–91, Kidderminster lodged a protest. To their delight, the protest was upheld by the FA and the match replayed. This time Darwen won 13–0!

SMASHING NEWS

Jonathan Gould, son of Coventry City boss Bobby, chose an unusual way to mark the fact that he would be taking over in goal for the League match with Southampton on 3 April 1993. Within two hours of hearing the good news, he had pranged his car twice. He reflected: 'I hope that's all my bad luck out of the way in one go.' Two weeks later, Liverpool put four past him at Anfield.

SHOW ME THE WAY TO GO HOME

Having drowned their sorrows in a bar in Cologne where their team Celtic had just lost 2–0 in a September 1992 UEFA Cup tie, soccer fans George and Pat were tired and wanted to go to bed. They hailed a taxi driver and ordered, 'Take us to our hotel.' A slight hitch was that not only couldn't the pair remember the name of the hotel, they couldn't even remember which town it was in. After careful consideration, they plumped for Dortmund, some 90 miles away. A £70 cab fare later, the boys were broke and no nearer finding the elusive accommodation. Then at 3am they had a brainwave – they rang Pat's wife in Scotland. She knew the hotel's number and the area code revealed it was another 70 miles away in Dusseldorf. Well, it began with a D. The police then organized a whip-round so that our intrepid explorers could pay their way back to Dusseldorf.

8-MINUTE WONDER

It is every player's dream to be picked for his country and West Ham United's Jimmy Barrett was no exception. But after just eight minutes of his international debut against Northern Ireland on 19 October 1929, Barrett was injured and carried off. He was never picked again and holds the dubious distinction of having the shortest England career.

PHONE GOAL

Queen's Park Rangers supremo Richard Thompson scored a £335 own goal when he rang his team's Clubcall line. After listening to the latest news about the Rangers on a car phone, he did not replace the handset correctly. The following morning when he went to get into his car ready to drive in to work, he heard manager Gerry Francis's voice still talking. The call ended up costing Thompson £335 but as he said: 'Fortunately most of the money will come back to QPR.'

BIN THE PINK

Desperate times call for desperate measures. So Torquay United, languishing in the lower reaches of the Third Division during season 1992–93 and finding themselves unable to improve matters on the field, decided to try a little psychology off it. Nothing as drastic as lifting a curse or parading the club's past trophies before every game (a very short ceremony), instead they opted to paint the away team dressing room 'sleepy' pink. The idea was that visiting sides would be lulled into tranquility by the peaceful pastel shades and on taking the field would be rendered impotent in the face of a tidal wave of warrior-like United attacks. But the colour scheme merely seemed to make United's opponents more determined and following four quick home defeats, the Devon club thought it wise to redecorate. 'The pink just didn't seem to have the desired effect,' lamented a club official.

TREBLE TROUBLE

*F*ormer St. Mirren captain Billy Abercrombie boasts the distinction of having been sent off three times in the same match, against Motherwell in 1986. Referee Louis Thow brandished the red card at Abercrombie three times – first for the original offence, the second for talking back and the final one for dissent. Abercrombie was banned for 12 matches.

FOUR OFF

*Towards the end of a Third Division match at Northampton
on 6 September 1992, spectators could be heard placing
bets on how many players visiting Hereford would end up
with. The lucky ones were those who chose seven. The first
Hereford man to be sent off by referee Brian Coddington was
Andy Theodosiou after a 72nd-minute foul. Two minutes
later, assistant coach Greg Downs followed for protesting
about the award of a penalty to the home side. With the
score at 1–1, the nine men having equalized the penalty,
Hereford's numbers were reduced to eight when David
Titterton was dismissed for time-wasting. Then in the final
minute, Richard Jones was despatched for a foul to complete
a quartet of sendings-off in just 18 minutes. Clearly Hereford
had developed a taste for the proverbial early bath since on
his first game back after suspension, Titterton was sent off
again, in the fixture with Wrexham. A club official
admitted: 'Our discipline could have been better.'*

LOSING STREAK

Stockport United FC of the Stockport Football League
managed to lose 39 consecutive League and Cup
matches between September 1976 and 18 February 1978.
When this splendid run came to an end, it was said that
players and officials didn't know whether to laugh or cry.

MOTSON BEWARE!

The subtle interviewing technique of Peruvian broadcaster
Mario Sanchez spectacularly failed to endear him to his
subject following a match in Lima. Ramming a microphone
under the nose of 6ft 3in striker Corina, Sanchez asked him

why he had missed three simple heading chances and how he thought that area of his game could be improved. Corina pondered for a moment and then announced, 'like this' before head-butting his inquisitor in the face, rendering him unconscious. Corina was arrested after a scuffle with police.

CLASSIC OWN GOAL

In a First Division game at Derby on 24 October 1992, visitors Charlton showed the value of teamwork to create a classic strike on goal. The ball was languishing idly around the half-way line when suddenly two touches, neither from a Derby player, left the ball nestling in the back of the Charlton net. First, Charlton's Darren Pitcher succeeding in slicing the loose ball high into the air and 30 yards back towards his own goal. Still there was no immediate danger, but as the ball plummeted from orbit just outside the

penalty area, team-mate Scott Minto intervened to place the deftest of headers wide of advancing keeper Bob Bolder and into the corner of the net. Many of the spectators thought it was worth the admission money alone.

SOMETHING FISHY

In days of yore, it was the practice after testimonial matches at Grimsby for players to be given cases of fish as thanks for their participation. After one such game, Tom Finney was presented with a case of plaice and Nat Lofthouse received a case of cod. Lofthouse queried this and asked the donor: 'How come Finney's got plaice and I've only got cod?' The man replied: 'Well he played better than you did tonight.'

BOSTON STUMPED

At the start of the 1992–93 season, Boston United officials discovered that the new back-pass rule was proving a costly business. As defenders tried to boot their way out of trouble, two match balls worth £40 apiece were kicked over the stand at their York Street ground never to be seen again.

GONE WEST

Manchester United's Enoch West was banned for life when he was found guilty, with other players, of fixing the result of a match with Liverpool on 2 April 1915. Because of their distinguished war records, his co-conspirators had their bans lifted after the First World War but West's remained in force for 30 years until 1945. When it was eventually lifted, he was 62 and wisely decided against a comeback.

KICKING THE HABIT

It doesn't say much for the footballing prowess of Italian celebrities that they felt compelled to object to the opposing team's strip – particularly since their opponents, Reggio Emilia, are a team of monks! Prior to kick-off, the celebrity XI bitterly complained about the monks' insistence on wearing their traditional habits for the match. One celebrity moaned later: 'It wasn't fair. The habit makes it impossible to put the ball through their legs.' In front of a crowd of 14,000, the team with God on their side won 4–3.

FASTEST SENDING-OFF

That honour rests with Bologna's Giuseppe Lorenzo who, after a mere ten seconds of the Italian League match with Parma on 9 December 1990, was dismissed for striking an opponent. Neither does our own Vinny Jones exactly hang

around when it comes to incurring the wrath of officialdom.
Playing for Sheffield United away to Manchester City in
January 1991, he managed to get himself booked five seconds
after the kick-off. But the following year, now wearing a
Chelsea shirt, Jones broke his personal best with a splendid
booking after just three seconds of the Cup tie with his old
team-mates from Bramall Lane. Such was Jones' speed off the
mark that the ball hadn't even left the centre circle before he
launched himself into a reckless tackle.

A TOUCH OF THE SPRAKES

Copying professional goalkeepers is an admirable trait
but is less desirable when you inadvertantly recreate
Gary Sprake's biggest blunder. Vaughan Tucker, a local
league custodian from Lytham St. Annes, had just made
what he called 'the greatest save of my life' in diving
full-length to hold a penalty. Sadly, this feat of
athleticism did not have a happy ending. 'My team-
mates were still applauding me,' said Vaughan, 'as I got
up and went to throw the ball out to the wing. But
instead it slipped out of my hand and into the net. And I
got thrown out of the team.'

INSIDE, RIGHT!

*After reaching their local cup final, to take place on a
neutral ground, prison team Lags XI from Holme House
jail in Stockton, Cleveland, were kicked out because they
could only play at home. Their manager moaned: 'The
players asked if they could be let out with Group 4
guarding them, but were refused.'*

TALK OF THE TOWN

In 1986 Buckingham Town's centre-forward was arrested by police ten minutes before an FA Cup tie, mid-way through the team-talk!

WRETCHED ROCHDALE

Rochdale have two claims for an entry into the footballing hall of fame. One of their players, John Burns, was sent off on his debut against Stockport County on 29 October 1921 and ten years later, on 7 November 1931, they overcame New Brighton 3–2 before setting off on a crowd-pleasing run of 17 straight League defeats. They didn't taste even the sweet success of a draw until 9 March 1932 when New Brighton once again volunteered to play them and charitably drew 1–1.

CRICKET

EXPENSIVE DELIVERY

The stage was set for an enthralling encounter between Western Australians, Bunbury and a visiting touring team from Victoria. Bunbury's opening bowler steamed in to deliver the first ball of the match...which was promptly despatched into a three-pronged branch of a tall Jarrah tree. And there it sat. The home side desperately claimed that it was a lost ball, but the umpire decreed that it was not lost because it could be seen, those being the quaint rules in days of old. Meanwhile, the Victoria batsmen continued to run. By now the Bunbury players were beside themselves. They tried to resort to drastic measures by sending for an axe to fell the tree but none could be found. Finally, someone produced a rifle and the ball was shot down from its perch. Alas, by the time it had been returned to the middle, the batsmen had run 286. It will come as no surprise to learn that Victoria went on to win comfortably.

ILLUSTRIOUS CAREER

When the names of great Australian cricketers are under discussion, for some reason it is always the likes of Bradman, Benaud and Lillee that spring to the fore. Only rarely does that of Dr. R.L. Park warrant a mention. Perhaps this is because in his solitary Test appearance against England at Melbourne in 1920, the hapless medic was out

first ball in his only innings and delivered a solitary over
which cost his side nine runs. He was said to be disappointed
at not being selected again.

LAMBS TO THE SLAUGHTER

*F*acing a target of 133, Seaham Harbour were skittled for just
one run by Gateshead Fell in the Durham Under-18
League...and even that came from a leg bye. It was a case of
trial by ordeal as Seaham, some of whose batsmen were only
11, wilted in the face of a furious onslaught launched by 16-
year-olds Neil Killeen and Steve Lugsden, both Durham
county players who have appeared in Gateshead Fell's first
team. Nine of the youngsters were clean bowled and the tenth
was run out, making a rare sortie from the crease, as the
Seaham innings lasted a mere nine overs. It was thought that
he had simply been trying to escape to the safety of the
pavilion. Shortly before proceedings came to a merciful
climax, two brave souls had successfully ventured down the
wicket to scamper a leg bye, much to the disgust of
Gateshead's demonic duo. Steve Lugsden moaned: 'I was
upset when they got their run – I wanted to get them out for
nothing.' Seaham secretary Jim Dyson said of the debacle in
May 1993: 'It was sheer terror for most of our lads. Some were
so scared they almost stood beside the square leg umpire as
the bowlers ran in!'

BROKE HIS DUCK

*I*n 1990, Northamptonshire tail-ender Mark Robinson had
enjoyed a less than glorious summer with the bat. From
4 May he went 12 first-class innings without scoring a run
until finally on 15 September, he rounded off the season with
a magnificent 1 not out which played no small part in

helping his side to victory over Leicestershire. Suggestions that the run was a gift were hastily dismissed and Robinson, cheered all the way back to the pavilion, declared: 'It was one of the proudest moments of my life.'

GREEN'S HOUSE EFFECT

When Walsden entertained Rochdale in a Central Lancashire League match, Walsden bowler Peter Green was hit for a massive six by Rochdale batsman Wilson Hartley. The ball sailed out of the ground and smashed through the window of a house in an adjoining street. To add insult to injury, it was Peter Green's house.

SHORTEST MATCH

A supposed friendly between a team of Fijians and Europeans, the latter under the captaincy of the Hon. J.A. Udal, on the island of Taveuni in 1906 was abandoned after just one ball had been bowled. It had dismissed the local High Chief who was so irate at being out that it was deemed prudent not to proceed further with the game.

WORST TEST FIGURES

The distinction of achieving the worst bowling figures in Test match history goes to the hitherto unsung L.O.B. 'Chuck' Fleetwood-Smith, an Australian left-arm spinner. Playing against England at the Oval in 1938, his sustained spell didn't exactly succeed in tying the home bats men down. England declared at 903–7 and Fleetwood-Smith finished with the highly forgettable figures of 1–298.

TOO SMALL FOR HIS BOOTS

Even the greatest of players have their off days. Take Denis Compton about to make his MCC debut against Suffolk at Felixstowe. Later renowned for being not exactly the most organized of individuals, young Compton arrived at the ground to discover that he had left his cricket bag at Lord's. Consequently, he was obliged to take the field in kit borrowed from a player seven inches taller than himself and who took two-and-a-half-boot sizes larger. The suspicion that Compton would have been more comfortable in a suit of armour was reinforced when, scarcely able to move about the crease, he was not altogether surprisingly bowled first ball.

OUT OF POCKET

Village teams can always rely on special fund-raising matches to acquire essential extra revenue for ground maintenance. Thus in 1989, Twyford CC near Bristol staged

*just such a fixture which brought in a much-needed £44.
Unfortunately in the course of the match a window was
broken by a six and the club had to fork out £45 to repair it!*

SWIFT DEPARTURE

Informed sources tell of the occasion when Henry Tubb
of Free Foresters and Oxford University swung a
mighty blow which looked to be going clean out of the
ground until it struck a swift in flight and rebounded
into the hands of a surprised fielder.

TURNING A DEAF EAR

The First Test between England and Australia at Trent
Bridge in 1953 saw Australia floundering at 81–6 in their
second innings. The evening gloom was gathering over
Nottingham and so as Don Tallon, Australia's wicket-keeper
who was known to be hard of hearing, left the pavilion to bat,
his captain Lindsay Hassett shouted after him: 'Deafy, give

the light a go,' meaning that Tallon should appeal against the light. However Tallon mis-heard the instructions as 'have a go' and proceeded to launch into an inexplicable and frenzied attack upon the English bowling before holing out for a quick-fire 15 while attempting another big hit. Australia were duly bowled out for 123 but, despite Tallon's efforts, managed to hold on for a draw.

TOO DRUNK TO BOWL

Yorkshire and England left-arm spinner Bobby Peel was booted out of the game in the 1890s by his county captain Lord Hawke after Peel had walked on to the field too drunk to know in which direction he was supposed to be bowling. Hawke, a disciplinarian who would have made Cromwell seem the life and soul of the party, later explained by way of absolution: 'It had to be done for the sake of discipline and for the good of cricket.'

BURNT OUT

Batting at Kalgoorlie, Australia, in the 1970s, one Stan Dawson was struck by a speedy delivery that promptly ignited a box of matches which he had secreted in his hip pocket. To add to his woe, Dawson was run out as he tried to beat down the flames.

DISMISSED HIMSELF

Tailender James Southerton insisted he was out during a match at The Oval in 1870 and stalked off while the umpire tried to call him back. It went into the scorebook as 'J. Southerton, retired thinking he was out.'

OUT ON BAIL?

When England toured Australasia in 1877, they were horrified to learn that the First Test in Melbourne was to take place virtually as soon as they had disembarked after the boat crossing from New Zealand. As it was, half of the team took the field suffering from sea-sickness while their only wicket-keeper, Edward Pooley, was languishing in a Christchurch jail. Before one of the matches played in New Zealand, he had struck up a bet with a local gambler as to how many Christchurch batsmen would score ducks. Pooley reckoned he was owed nearly £9 but the gambler welshed on the deal. The resulting argument ended in fisticuffs and both men were jailed pending a trial. By the time Pooley was acquitted, his team-mates had lost the First Test by 45 runs.

OF LITTLE BENEFIT

A benefit match has always been the icing on the cake for professional cricketers, a fitting reward for years of sterling service. So naturally Somerset's Bertie Buse was eagerly anticipating his chosen fixture, against Lancashire in 1953, in the hope that the weather would stay fine for the three days and thus bring out the crowds. Before the match, actor Arnold Ridley (later of Dad's Army fame) wrote in an open letter to Buse: 'Good luck to your benefit. May you score plenty of runs and get busy among the wickets.' But, disastrously for Buse's pocket, he got a little too busy among the wickets, contributing to his own downfall by removing six Lancashire batsmen. As a result, the game was all over in a day with Somerset taking advantage of an awkward pitch to triumph by an innings and 24 runs. So whilst expressing sympathy for Buse, it has to be said that it was something of a self-inflicted wound.

MORBID SCORECARD

Playing in the final of the 1958–59 Qaid-I-Azam Trophy in
Karachi, Abdul Aziz was injured in the first innings. The
scorecard thus read: 'Abdul Aziz retired hurt...0.' The injury
proved to be fatal and the scorer, obviously not wishing to
leave any room for doubt, wrote for the second innings:
'Abdul Aziz did not bat, dead...0'.

HASTY EXIT

England's 1959–60 tour of the West Indies was marred
by disgraceful riot scenes in Port of Spain. Bottles and
seats were hurled onto the pitch, observed by the keen
eye of BBC radio commentator Rex Alston. 'I've never
seen anything like it in my life,' he broadcast. 'The
crowd away to my right are behaving like a lot of
hooligans.' Unfortunately for Alston, the said crowd
were tuned in to his commentary on their transistor
radios and on hearing his words of condemnation, they
turned towards the derelict commentary box in anger.
Alston and his colleagues were forced to flee to safety as
the old box was reduced to a pile of rubble in little more
than 30 seconds.

ONE-BALL DEFEAT

Spectators assembled for the York Senior League fixture
between Cawood and Dringhouses in August 1979
expecting a closely-fought contest. But it looked rather
ominous for Dringhouses when their entire team were
bowled out for just 2. Hopes of similar reprisals proved
remarkably short-lived since the first delivery of Cawood's
reply flew past the wicket-keeper for four byes. Thus

Cawood had won without actually hitting a ball.
A Dringhouses player conceded that 'probably the better
team won on the day.'

SOUVENIR HUNTER

When England toured Australia in 1886–87, they were supposed to be playing a Combined Australia XI at Melbourne. However, the leading lights of New South Wales were not available so instead the English and Victorian teams were divided up into Smokers and Non-Smokers and a match was arranged between them. This contrived spectacle proved of absolutely no interest whatsoever to the Melbourne public, the attendance on the final day barely reaching 100. It was so forgettable that Victoria's W.H. Scotton, who was batting at the time, decided he would like the match ball as a souvenir of the occasion. At the end of play he picked it up, only to be given out by a fussy umpire (probably one who had just given up smoking) as 'handled ball'.

IGUANA STOPPED PLAY

The First Test between Young Sri Lanka and Young England in 1987 was briefly halted when a large iguana crept sinisterly across the square at the Colombo Cricket Club ground.

NO-WIN SITUATION

Centuries are far too commonplace to be remotely interesting, but one that would have been worthy of international acclaim was that attempted by

Northamptonshire in the late 1930s. Over four painstaking years, longer even than a Trevor Bailey hundred, Northants crawled their way towards a century of successive County Championship matches without a win. Their 'innings' began following victory over Somerset at Taunton on 14 May 1935 and continued effortlessly through their next 99 Championship fixtures (61 of them defeats). Then, agonisingly one short of their ton, they ended up beating Leicestershire by an innings in two days at Northampton on 29 May 1939.

UMPIRE CONFUSED

When Barbados met British Guiana in 1946, the umpires, accustomed to usually counting up to six, found great difficulty adjusting to the eight-ball over which was in force at the time. One over from Guiana's D.F. Hill, which contained neither wides nor no-balls, was allowed to continue unhindered for 14 deliveries. The umpire's miscalculation might have gone unnoticed had he had not given Everton Weekes out lbw to the 14th ball.

PRIDE BEFORE A FALL

It takes a team particularly adept in the art of failure to lose a match having bowled out the opposition for 15. But Warwickshire managed it with runs to spare in their County Championship fixture with Hampshire at Edgbaston in 1922. Having compiled a respectable 223 in their first innings, Warwickshire skittled the men from the south coast for a paltry 15. At the end of that first day, the Warwickshire captain, the Hon. F.S. Calthorpe, was naturally in bullish mood and suggested to his opposite number, the Hon. L.H. Tennyson, that when the match was over, the amateurs should play each other at golf. However, Tennyson was none too amused by the proposal and, apparently in language not appropriate to his social standing, he bet Calthorpe £10 that Hampshire would win the cricket match. Calthorpe must have thought he was on to easy money, only to see Hampshire, following-on, rattle up 521 and then bowl out Warwickshire for 158 in their second innings to gain an unlikely victory by 155 runs.

WICKETLESS

At Old Trafford in 1956, Leicestershire contrived to lose to Lancashire without taking a wicket in the entire match. Lancashire declared their first innings at 166–0 and knocked off the 66 required to wrap up a ten-wicket victory, again without being troubled by the feeble visiting attack.

BAD HAND SIGNALS

With his team batting, Ray East, the Essex Second XI coach, was sitting in the dressing-room when the phone rang. The call was for one of the Essex players, who could be seen in the distance meandering aimlessly around the boundary. Taking a leaf out of Lionel Blair's book, East mimed through the dressing-room door to get the player to the phone and then sat back in his chair again. Barely a minute had elapsed when instead of the wanted man, the two batsmen walked into the dressing-room. 'Lunch already, lads?' inquired East. 'No,' replied one, 'we've declared, haven't we? Wasn't that you waving us in?'

'QUICKEST' PAIR

Glamorgan's Peter Judge had an unfortunate experience at the hands of Indian bowler Sarwate when the tourists visited Cardiff. Last man in for the county, Judge was bowled first ball by Sarwate and, to save time when Glamorgan followed-on, he kept his pads on and stayed at the crease to open the second innings. Again, Judge was clean bowled by Sarwate first ball.

MISTAKEN IDENTITY

In 1899, Narraway's Farm at Acton was scheduled to be the venue for two matches. Kildare II were due to entertain Crescent of Hampstead while on an adjoining pitch, Kildare III were to meet Crofton from Streatham. But when the two visiting teams arrived, they each mistook the other for Kildare . The captains of Crescent and Crofton managed to exchange introductions without identifying themselves, tossed for first innings and the batsmen marched out to the middle. The first ball was about to be bowled when a Kildare player turned up and wondered why he didn't recognize any of his team-mates. When he passed on his concern to the umpires, proceedings were halted in the nick of time.

OFF THE OVER

*B*owling in a Queensland country match during season 1968–69, R. Grubb achieved the memorable feat of conceding 62 runs in one eight-ball over. Batsman H. Morley struck nine sixes and two fours off the over which included four no-balls.

CURIOUS DISMISSAL

*S*urrey opening batsman Laurie Fishlock was eager to capitalize on a no-ball which came his way during the match with Kent at the Oval in 1938. He advanced boldly down the wicket and launched himself into a full-blooded drive. Perhaps he overdid the aggression for as he swung at the ball, his bat snapped in two. Consequently, he got only the faintest of touches which carried through to the quick-thinking wicket-keeper who caught the ball and broke the wicket. A batsman cannot be out caught or stumped from a no-ball but Fishlock, with no bat to ground, had to return to the pavilion, adjudged run out.

GO SLOW

The noble game of cricket isn't just about frantic limited-over run chases – the science of stone-walling also has a valuable if unproductive part to play. The dead bat was witnessed at its finest during a Yorkshire League match between Green Hammerton, near York, and Headingley Broomfield in 1976. Set 181 to win, Green Hammerton had slumped to an alarming 14–8. It was fair to say that victory seemed unlikely so batsmen Tom Bell and Ken Kershaw decided to close ranks and bat out the remaining 75 minutes in the hope of securing a draw. Bell said later: 'We just put our heads down and we stopped.' While the spectators somehow managed to contain their excitement, the dour duo stayed through 33 successive maiden overs until Kershaw was finally prised out. In marched the last man, Mark Williams, but Bell, fearful that the newcomer might not even be able to block adequately, made the fatal mistake of trying to score a run in order to keep the strike. Attempting to scoop a single back over the bowler's head, Bell was caught and bowled by a Mr. Z. Ali who finished with the economical figures of 14–14–0–1. Green Hammerton had succumbed with just two minutes' playing time left. When the scorebook was examined, it revealed that there were 288 balls in the Green Hammerton innings – and runs were scored from just eight.

TATE'S TORMENT

Few Test careers have been as miserable as that of 35-year-old Sussex bowler Fred Tate. Called up as a last-minute replacement against Australia at Old Trafford in 1902, he dropped a crucial catch, hardly bowled despite the wet conditions and had to go in last when England needed just eight runs to win. He made four but was then bowled, giving Australia victory by three runs. Poor Fred was never forgiven and it remained his one and only Test.

WASHOUT

Plans to stage an indoor cricket match at Basingstoke in 1993 were scuppered when the game was rained off. The pitch was flooded after water had poured through a hole in the sports hall roof.

LEAST SPORTING GESTURE

*P*assions ran high during the 1991 final of India's Duleep Trophy when West Zone bowler Rashid Patel aimed a head-high full toss at North Zone batsman Raman Lamba. The latter showed his displeasure, at which Patel uprooted a stump and attacked Lamba with it. Mercifully, this sort of cricketing vandalism is usually confined to a hot day on Blackpool beach.

UNSUCCESSFUL EXPERIMENT

*S*ometimes in the field of sport, it really does pay to stick to what you do best, a fact to which Glamorgan's Malcolm Nash would surely testify. A 23-year-old fast medium left-arm bowler of some promise, Nash decided to experiment with a slower style against Nottinghamshire at Swansea on 31 August 1968. Notts' West Indian Test star Garfield Sobers responded by hitting each of Nash's deliveries for six, taking a maximum 36 off the over. Nash remained philosophical, conceding: 'I suppose I can gain some consolation from the fact that my name will be permanently in the record books.'

MEMORABLE CAREER

If Gloucestershire batsman Sidney George Wells had ever recounted tales of his cricketing life in print, it would have been a slim volume indeed. For his exploits in the first-class game were a tableau of inactivity – in fact it is questionable whether he actually set foot on the pitch. Sidney's career consisted of just one appearance, against Kent at Bristol in 1927, but the match was abandoned without a ball being bowled!

MIS-MATCH OF THE DAY

Dera Ismail Khan knew they faced stiff opposition when taking on Pakistan Western Railways in an Ayub Trophy match at Lahore in December 1964 but even they couldn't have expected it to turn out quite so one-sided. Batting first, Railways piled up the runs and occupied the crease until lunch on the third day at which point they declared at 910–6. After so long in the field and faced with a veritable mountain to climb even to save the follow-on, perhaps it was inevitable that Dera Ismail Khan should wilt. And wilt they did. They were rapidly bowled out for 32 and 27 to go down by the fairly conclusive margin of an innings and 851 runs. It was Dera Ismail Khan's first and last first-class match.

THE UPS AND DOWNS OF CRICKET

Contemporary reports tell of a fine game of cricket played at Chatham Lines, Kent, back in the 1880s. One side amassed a moderately respectable 46, only for their opponents to win with a single hit. The lucky strike sent the ball rolling down to the foot of a steep hill known as the Brook. A posse of fielders set off in pursuit and positioned themselves along the hillside, the idea being that they would throw the ball to each other in relays prior to returning it to the middle. However, the tactic ended in abysmal failure as some of the relay catchers had an unfortunate tendency to drop the ball, at which point it rolled back down to the bottom of the hill. While this lengthy retrieval process was being effected, the batsmen were trotting up and down at their leisure to compile the 47 runs necessary for victory. A similar tale comes from a match played on Beacon Hill near the Sussex village of Rottingdean where no fewer than 67 runs were scored off a single hit. The ball raced down the hill to the village where again a relay system of fielders set about organizing its rapid return. But these players had much safer hands and the conveyer belt looked to be doing a competent job until they were let down in spectacular fashion by the last man in the line. It was his task to throw the ball in to the wicket-keeper, but tragically his return was too high and the keeper could only look on in anguish as the ball sailed over his head and rolled down the other side of the hill...

SAD DISMISSAL

Playing against Somerset at Taunton on 22 May 1919, Sussex's H.J. Heygate was given out because he failed to reach the crease within two minutes of the fall of the previous wicket. Poor Heygate was crippled with rheumatism and couldn't make it to the middle when the ninth Sussex wicket fell in their second innings. He was shown on the scorecard as 'absent'.

EIGHT MEN SHORT

Kent were all set to take the field for the second day of their County Championship match with Middlesex at Tunbridge Wells in June 1963 when they realized that only three of the Middlesex team were present. The rest had been stuck in heavy traffic. The trio were one batsman who was not out, one who had already been out and the 12th man. The not out player, Bob White, thought he might as well get padded up and wait in the middle in the hope that a partner might soon arrive. With the Kent fielders idling their time looking for someone to bowl to, the umpires decided they could wait no longer and officially closed the Middlesex innings. Kent then came out to bat ten minutes later with many of their number being temporarily loaned to Middlesex as fielders. Indeed one, Prodger, standing at second slip, had the distinction of catching his own team-mate Brian Luckhurst! The fun ended when the other Middlesex players turned up and it settled down to another routine county game.

PLUCK OF THE IRISH

*T*he proudest day in the annals of Irish cricket spectacularly coincided with just about the most humiliating one in the history of the West Indies. In 1969, fielding six of the team which had drawn the previous day's Test with England (including the likes of Clive Lloyd, Basil Butcher, Joey Carew and John Shepherd), the West Indies were skittled for 25 by Ireland in a one-day match at Londonderry. It could have been even worse for at one point the West Indies were 12–9. Ireland went on to complete a memorable nine-wicket victory. The steel bands were silent that night.

GONE TO LUNCH

W hen Sussex entertained Kent at Brighton in August 1891, the lunchtime fare provided at the ground apparently held little appeal for the gourmet palate of the visitors' C.J.M. Fox, so he went elsewhere for lunch. He partook of such a sumptuous repast that by the time he had returned to the action, the Kent innings had ended and he had been given out 'absent'.

THREE DUCKS IN ONE MATCH

It is no mean feat to be dismissed three times in a match without scoring but what makes this particular deed of incompetence all the more praiseworthy is that it happened to none other than Viv Richards. Even at the tender age of 18, Richards was worshipped by cricket-lovers in Antigua. And the crowd were looking forward to another peerless display from the youngster when he walked to the crease to face St. Kitts in the 1969 Leeward Islands Tournament at Antigua Recreation Ground. So imagine their disgust when he was given out fourth ball to a dubious bat-pad catch. Never ones to hide their emotions, the Antiguan spectators promptly brought the match to a halt. The umpires, appreciating the delicate nature of the situation, amazingly agreed to give Antigua's favourite son another chance. Richards duly re-emerged...but was soon out stumped. This time there was no controversy. Nor was there in the second innings when he was again out for nought to complete a treble failure.

CONSISTENTLY BAD

A cricket club from North-East Lancashire calling themselves The Untouchables established a splendid sequence of ineptitude between 1945 and 1956. In the course of those 12 seasons, they played 127 games and never once managed to register a win. They lost 109 and drew the remainder. On one occasion when they needed just nine runs to win with six wickets standing and victory at last appeared within their grasp, they sensibly collapsed in the nick of time to ensure that their record remained intact.

NEW ZEALAND'S FINEST HOUR

The gallant batsmen of New Zealand wrote their way into the record books with a stunning display of inefficiency in the Second Test against England at Eden Park, Auckland, on 28 March 1955. It had all started tediously enough. In their first innings New Zealand made an adequate 200 and England replied with 246. Little could the tourists have known that such a slender lead would be sufficient for them not to have to bat again. For when New Zealand took to the crease second

time around, they were routed for an all-time Test record low of 26 in just 27 overs. Sadly, the symmetry of the scorecard was spoiled by one thoughtless soul reaching double figures.

WASTED JOURNEY

Many celebrities are ardent cricketers and film star Trevor Howard was certainly among that number. But even he must have later queried the merits of agreeing to appear in a match at Buxton, Derbyshire, on 27 July 1960. To take part, he got up at 5am and then travelled 180 miles from his home to Buxton...only to be caught at the wicket first ball.

TEN-DAY DRAW

With England one up in the 1939 series in South Africa, the final Test at Durban in March was crucial. Since the rubber was at stake, it was decreed that the match should be played to a finish. On and on it went for nine long days with proceedings being dominated by the batsmen. It had been agreed that the tenth day would be the last since the England team had to catch their ship home from Cape Town and there was no other boat for two weeks. But there seemed little prospect of a result until on that last afternoon, England launched a spectacular victory charge, reaching the stage where they needed just 42 runs for victory with five wickets standing. Then it rained...and didn't stop. After 43 hours of play, the match was abandoned as a draw. The South African Board of Control issued a statement at 5.45pm saying that, in consultation with the captains, they 'agreed that the match should be abandoned, the Board recognizing that the MCC would otherwise not have the requisite number of hours in Cape Town before sailing home.'

DEVON DUMB

Minor County Devon surpassed the expectations of all but their most cynical followers when slipping up by 346 runs in a 1990 Nat-West Trophy tie at Torquay. Somerset rattled up a record-breaking 413–4 dec. in their 60 overs. In reply, Devon could muster just 67. Most of the team were left speechless but Devon captain Hiley Edwards, calling Torquay a 'postage stamp ground', claimed: 'Even mishits were going for six. But we were pleased Somerset played the game properly and used no occasional bowlers. We wanted no charity and they gave us none.' He added defiantly: 'I must admit our players are a bit cheesed off at the moment but our defeat by 346 runs will do us no harm.'

HAMBLEDONGATE

In the days before scoreboards, the method for keeping totals was to cut a notch on a stick for every run and to make every tenth notch longer. Under this primitive calculation, Kent's match with Hambledon at Windmill Down in July 1783 was declared a tie. But it was later discovered that in one place the scorer had inadvertantly marked the 11th notch instead of the tenth. It seemed that Kent had justifiable claims for victory and indeed the faulty stick was produced in evidence. However, in what smacks of a cover-up, it was reported that 'the other scorer could not or would not produce his.'

WORST TEST BATSMAN

Few wielders of the willow could compete with Indian spinner Bhagwat Chandrasekhar who usually dealt with pace bowling from a position adjacent to the square leg umpire. In view of his timerity, it is hardly surprising that he managed four 'pairs' in Test matches.

TEACHER KNOWS BEST

*I*n 1989, ten-year-old Zac Morris was proving more than a handful for Derby under-11s . The Barnsley schoolboy took no fewer than five wickets in his first over but, allegedly in the interests of fairness, was then barred from bowling by the teachers. No doubt the Derby teachers were especially keen on this decisive action, particularly since their team went on to win. Whether the Barnsley masters had some explaining to do later I know not, but such a magnanimous gesture would surely be a boon if introduced to the first-class game. Think how we could have prospered over the years if we had persuaded the Australians to stop Lillee from bowling because he was too quick for our batsmen.

BROTHERLY INFLUENCE

There is more than a hint of suspicion that Australian Test star George Giffen used his influence to get his brother Walter a game. Certainly Walter's on-field achievements did nothing to suggest that he was worthy of inclusion in the national line-up. Picked as an opening batsman, Walter burst up on the scene with 2 and 0 in his debut against England at Sydney in 1887. For a while he was deservedly consigned to the wilderness, only to be recalled for two Tests against W.G. Grace's tourists in 1891–92. Showing no loss of form whatsoever, Walter responded with knocks of 1, 3, 3 and 2. That would have sounded the death knell for most batsmen yet even with an average of 1.83, Walter was chosen for the 1893 touring side. Mysteriously, the selectors overlooked him when choosing the actual Test teams and so this fine cricketer was prevented from inflicting any further damage on England's attack.

NO-BALL SENTIMENTS

*W*ith England completing their victory over South Africa in the 1960 Lord's Test just after lunch on the fourth day, it was decided to arrange an exhibition match between the two teams. Far from being a harmless friendly, it once again brought to the surface doubts about the bowling action of South Africa's Geoff Griffin who, during the Test itself, had been no-balled for throwing 11 times by square leg umpire Frank Lee. If Griffin thought all that would be forgotten in the exhibition match, he was sorely mistaken. He only bowled one over – and it lasted 11 deliveries. This time it was Lee's fellow umpire, Sid Buller, who called no-ball for four out of Griffin's first five deliveries. Possibly attempting to defuse the situation, South African captain Jackie McGlew suggested to Griffin that he should bowl the remainder of the over underarm. Surely even Griffin couldn't be no-balled for that. But he was. Frank Lee promptly declared his next delivery void because Griffin had failed to warn the batsman that he was switching from overarm to underarm!

FINE LEG WORE A THREE-PIECE SUIT

A match between Yorkshire and Derbyshire at Dewsbury in 1899 was not so much affected by rain as by water in general. At the end of the second day, a mini torrent seeped through the ceiling and into the Derbyshire dressing-room after someone had left the taps on in the catering department above. Most of the players' kit was ruined, causing a hasty reappraisal of team responsibilities when Derbyshire fielded. The two players whose playing gear was relatively unscathed were forced to bowl while the other nine took to the field in their best suits. Yorkshire, who needed only 32 to win at the start of the third day, wasted no time in knocking off the required runs, the fielders being somewhat reluctant to end up with grass stains on their Sunday finery.

EXTRA HELP

Thoughtfully offering assistance to their opponents' total, the West Indies conceded a handsome 71 extras in Pakistan's first innings at Georgetown, Guyana, in April 1988. Of these, 38 were no-balls and 21 were byes. The following January in a one-day international at Brisbane, again with Pakistan, the West Indies were once more generous to a fault, giving away 59 extras, 37 of them wides.

NEVER SCORED A RUN

Over the years many claims have been advanced with regard to the world's worst batsman but one individual deserving of the most serious consideration is Somerset's A.H.S. Clark whose number of initials comfortably outscored his first-class run total. His career was confined to the summer of 1930 when in nine innings he failed to trouble the scorer on any occasion. His detractors point to the fact that he was not out a couple of times but fail to realize that, given his overall record, even if he had stayed at the crease, the outcome would surely have been the same.

WRONG LABEL

Although situated in neighbouring Wiltshire, it was deemed a good idea to stage one of Gloucestershire's 1988 Sunday League fixtures at Swindon. However, the masterplan had to be shelved when the square at Swindon became totally bald. It transpired that during the winter, weedkiller had been accidentally applied to the pitch instead of fertilizer.

BREAKDOWN IN COMMUNICATIONS

Even as fine a player as former Australian captain Bobby Simpson has had moments he might rather forget. Leading Australia in a country match in South Africa, he forgot to tell the opposing skipper that, with a lead of almost 450, he wished to enforce the follow-on. As a result, at the end of the tea interval, both teams came out to field!

HANGING ON THE TELEPHONE

The invention of the mobile phone has already begun to have an adverse effect on the peaceful world of village cricket. In 1989 it was reported that a game between Burridge in Hampshire and a Yorkshire touring team was regularly interrupted by the Burridge players' portable telephones. Indeed a number of misfields were put down to players trying to stop the ball with one hand while the phone was pressed to their ear with the other.

THREE OUT OFF ONE BALL

A match between Yorkshire Colts and Northants 2nd XI at Barnsley on 25 May 1958 produced a comi-tragic chain of events, the like of which is a rarity even in the eccentric world of English cricket. It all began when Yorkshire's Ted Lester lofted a shot to deep extra cover where fielders Jim Edmonds and Mick Norman, their eyes on the skies, unwittingly competed for the catch. It was an accident just waiting to happen. The crowd were not disappointed as Edmonds held on to the ball and in the process was knocked unconscious in a collision with Norman. For his part, Norman was concussed and, his leg spiked by Edmonds' boot, he was carted off to hospital. Edmonds subsequently recovered but the havoc caused by that single shot read: One laid out, one taken out and one given out.

THE STING

Going out to bat for Middlesex at Lord's, Patsy Hendren was half-way to the wicket when he flung his bat in the air, let out a piercing shriek and scampered back to the pavilion. He had a wasp in his box!

INJURY CRISIS

The Indian batsmen found themselves on the receiving end of some hostile West Indian bowling in the 1976 Test at Kingston, Jamaica. Gaekwad, Viswanath and Patel all retired hurt in the first innings and then Bedi and Chandrasekhar were both injured fielding. The last pair might not have been too worried about not having to face the West Indian attack again but it did mean that in their second innings, India had only six batsmen. Consequently they slumped from 97–2 to 97 all out, leaving the West Indies just 13 to win. Bedi later described the match as 'a war'.

ALL OUT FOR 0

There have been sundry instances of entire teams being dismissed without scoring but surely one of the most catastrophic was that of the Electrical Trades Commercial Travellers Association CC who were routed by Surrey villagers Bookham on 22 June 1952. What made matters worse was that Bookham needed just one ball to overhaul their opponents since the first delivery of their reply sailed through for four byes.

PREMATURE CELEBRATION

Leicestershire had been having a torrid time in the field in recent matches, spilling a number of catches, much to the disgust of their skipper Ray Illingworth. One Sunday against Derbyshire, Ashley Harvey-Walker skied a ball from Illingworth to deep mid-wicket where it was safely caught by David Gower. In a combination of relief and jubilation, Gower hurled the ball into the air. But his joy was curtailed by a swift rebuke from Illingworth, ordering him to throw it back since it was a no-ball. By the time the ball had descended from the heavens, the ricochet enabled them to run yet again although observers say that by this time the batsmen were so helpless with laughter that they were scarcely capable of standing up let alone running. The upshot of it all was that three runs came from a no-ball. Illingworth was not amused.

SOAP BAG

It is rumoured that a number of club cricketers play the game simply so that they can get away from their wives for a few hours. But there was no escape for one poor soul taking part in a match at Howick, South Africa, in March 1958. His wife telephoned the ground and insisted on speaking to him even though he was batting at the time. Thus the match was held up while he dashed to the pavilion to deal with what was obviously an emergency. And the matter of life and death? She wanted to know what he had done with the soap!

CAN WE HAVE OUR BALL BACK?

On 27 June 1990, Derbyshire and Shropshire were about to take the field for their Nat-West Trophy match at Queen's Park, Chesterfield, when embarrassed officials suddenly realised something was missing – they had no cricket ball. Even the most dedicated cricketer finds it something of a handicap to play without a ball so players and umpires had to wait in the pavilion while the balls were rushed up the M1 from Derbyshire's county headquarters at Derby over 20 miles away. After a 45-minute delay, the tie finally got under way at 11.15 am. Derbyshire chief executive Bob Lark admitted: 'Somewhere along the line there has been a breakdown in communication, but no one is to blame – it's just one of those things.'

WICKET BEFORE LEGOVER

Cricket-mad Richard Baker cancelled his honeymoon to play a match in Ripon – and was bowled first ball.

UNHAPPY EXPERIENCE

It is fair to say that Surrey's 19-year-old right-handed batsman Frederick Buckle didn't really make his mark in the match with Middlesex at Lord's in July 1869. In the first innings, he was recorded as 'absent, not sent for in time – 0' and in the second innings as 'absent unwell – 0'. Without his assistance, Surrey lost by 43 runs.

KING FORCED TO ABDICATE

Facing a crucial Dewsbury and District League match with Upper Hopton in 1978, Wakefield club Calder Grove decided to ask West Indian Test player Collis King if he would turn out for them. So imagine Upper Hopton's horror when they discovered on their arrival the true identity of the player listed as C. King. The West Indian went on to make 94 as well as taking five wickets, two catches and running a man out. Not surprisingly, Upper Hopton, beaten by some 80 runs, lodged an objection and Calder Grove were fined £1 for fielding an ineligible player and were also made to forfeit the match. Their appeal vindicated, Upper Hopton should have been in conciliatory mood but there was more than a hint of bitterness from the club official who remarked: 'Calder Grove's ground is a dump, not a patch on ours. It has no gent's lavatory.'

YORKED!

Although some allowance must be made for the fact that they had one man absent ill, Northants weren't really at their best against Yorkshire at Northampton on 8 May 1908. So dismal was their performance that they were dismissed for 27 and 15 in just 2hrs 15mins.

NO BACKBONE

Spineless batsman Pieter Marrish forfeited his wicket in a game at Johannesburg in 1972 because he spotted a snake and was too frightened to return to the crease. Meanwhile the wicket-keeper, obviously a man of steel, had ample time to remove the bails and stump him.

THE HAND OF GIL

On the eve of the 1956 Old Trafford Test, Australian wicket-keeper Gil Langley unaccountably ended up sleeping on his hand and caused so much damage to it that he was unable to play. Len Maddocks took his place but Australia should have known that it wasn't going to be their day. They were right, for this was the Test in which Jim Laker took his record-breaking 19 wickets. For the remainder of the tour a closer watch was kept on Langley's sleeping habits.

RUNNING JOKE

Luncarty's Jim McNichol greatly enlivened a Haig National Village tie with fellow Scots Manderston by running out three of his partners, including his captain, without facing a ball!

JACK WAS NO ACE

One of the briefest and least distinguished Ashes careers belonged to New South Wales opening batsman Jack Moroney who was chosen to play in one Test against England in 1950–51. In the first innings he lasted four balls until he was caught Hutton bowled Bailey from a leg glance but in the second innings he fared even worse, surviving just three deliveries before being leg before to Bailey. Moroney's Ashes career thus lasted seven balls and provided him with a pair.

WONDERFUL COLLAPSE

Few sights in sport are better than a total debacle. And that is the only way to describe the end of the Bond Worth innings in their Kidderminster League match with Cookley in July 1966. Already anticipating the glow of victory, Bond Worth were sitting pretty needing just three runs to win with five wickets standing. The deficit was further reduced when the first ball of the next over produced a single. But then in a lemming-like act of mass self-destruction, the next five balls saw the last five Bond Worth batsmen all run out, leaving Cookley the surprised winners by one run. As one Bond Worth player put it: 'I don't think our running between the wickets was as good as it could have been.'

TRUNCATED GAME

A group of boys were playing cricket at Earlwood, Sydney, in October 1962, watched from the boundary by an elephant from a nearby circus. When the ball was struck in its direction, the elephant fielded the ball with its trunk, swallowed it and ended the game.

UNSUNG HERO

One of the least auspicious cricketing careers was that of Joseph Emile Patrick McMaster who toured South Africa with Major Wharton's England team of 1888–89. McMaster batted at number nine, made a duck and wasn't called upon to bowl. And that was his solitary first-class game!

THE PERFECT GIFT

In 1989, Stuart Welch, an 18-year-old member of the MCC ground staff, won the search-for-a-spinner competition at Lord's. And the first prize was...a place on the MCC ground staff.

DIS-GUSTED

Former Warwickshire and England captain MJK Smith was facing a ball against Hampshire at Edgbaston in 1962 when a sudden gust of wind whipped his cap from his head. The headgear fell on to the stumps and he was given out 'hit wicket'.

THE PANE IS OVER

After 15 years without a win, the lads from Westmoreland Glass in Kendal, Cumbria, finally managed to scrape a three-run victory against a local cleaning firm. Hero bowler Mike Callan said: 'We could hardly believe it. We were thinking of arranging a game against an old folks' home just to get a win.'

LIFTING A THUMB

Fielding against Lancashire in July 1993, Leicestershire skipper Nigel Briers sprained a thumb when he caught it in his trouser pocket.

GOLF

SMALL MERCIES

Playing in the qualifying rounds for the 1965 Open, Walter Danecki from Milwaukee proved himself to be a golfer of quite exceptional ability. Forty-three-year-old Danecki, who had described himself on the entry form as a professional, began by recording 108 over the par 70 course at Hillside, Southport. The next day at Southport and Ainsdale, he took 113. Thus for the 36 holes, he had finished 81 over par and had the missed the qualifying total by 70 strokes. If it wasn't already obvious, it soon emerged that Walter wasn't a professional golfer at all. He had lied on the form. Why? 'Because I wanted that crock of gold.' Asked how he had enjoyed links golf, Walter unashamedly replied: 'Well I guess your small British ball helped me some. If I'd had to play the big ball, I'd have been all over the place.'

THE LEGEND OF MAURICE FLITCROFT

The exploits of Walter Danecki opened up a whole new world to rabbit golfers everywhere. Being able to take part in the Open (albeit only in the qualifying rounds) was like taking your own bat and ball to play at Lord's instead of in the park. Danecki may well have acted as inspiration for the headline-making deeds of Maurice Flitcroft, a 46-year-old crane driver from Barrow-in-Furness who took the Open by storm in 1976. Scarcely able to tame a crazy golf course let alone the windswept seaside links of Formby, Flitcroft

*returned a score of 121 in the first qualifying round. It
transpired that he had never before played a full 18 holes of
golf and, because he wasn't a member of any club, had been
forced to practice on the beach. The championship
committee were so aggrieved that they refunded the £30
entry fees to the two unfortunates drawn to play with him.
Flitcroft, who had only been playing golf in any shape or
form for 18 months, came back in 60 including a traumatic
11 at the 10th. Disappointed but better for the experience, he
said: 'I've made a lot of progress in the last few months and
I'm sorry I did not do better. I was trying too hard at the
beginning but began to put things together at the end of the
round.' But that was by no means the end of Maurice
Flitcroft. He re-surfaced in 1983, calling himself Swiss
professional Gerald Hoppy, and returned a 63 for a
qualifying round for the Open at Pleasington. But before we
despair lest this great sporting failure had suddenly acquired
unsuspected prowess, it should be pointed out the 63 was for
nine holes. At that point, a vigilant Royal and Ancient
official politely but firmly suggested that Herr Hoppy might
like to retire.*

HOW NOW?

Playing the 10th hole at Guernsey in 1963, golfer S.C. King
was safely on the fairway but his partner R.W. Clark was
lost in the rough. After helping him to look for the ball,
King returned to his own...and discovered a cow eating it.
Undaunted, the intrepid duo played again the following day.
This time the positions were reversed on the 10th and it
was King who was deep in the rough. Before joining the
search and remembering the events of the previous day,
Clark took precautions by placing his woollen hat over the
ball, predicting confidently: 'I'll make sure the cow doesn't
eat mine.' On his return, he found that the cow had eaten
his hat – although it had wisely declined to devour
the pom-pom.

WRONG TRAIN

A competitor heading for the 1922 Amateur Golf Championship at Prestwick boarded a train at Ayr, confident that it would be stopping at Prestwick. To his horror, the train sailed through the station and on towards Troon further along the coast. The track runs parallel to the first hole at Prestwick and the player screamed from the passing carriage that he would be back as soon as possible. On reaching Troon, he headed back post haste but it was all in vain – he had been disqualified, having missed his starting time.

TROD ON BALL

English golfer Roger Wethered was left to rue a careless lapse in the 1921 Open at St. Andrews – one which was to cost him the championship. Weighing up a shot to the 14th in the third round, Wethered was walking backwards when he accidentally trod on his ball, thus incurring a one-stroke penalty. How costly that one shot was for at the end of 72 holes he was left tied for first place with American 'Jock' Hutchison. And it was Hutchison who went on to win the play-off.

WHAT GOES UP...

There is nothing amiss with a little gentle exuberance to celebrate a moment of sporting glory. Thus it is perfectly acceptable to leap in the air after scoring a goal or to hurl the ball skywards having taken a catch at cricket but, as Bobby Cruickshank once discovered, it is unwise to attempt a similar feat with a golf club. Playing in the final round of the 1934 US Open at Merion, Cruickshank feared the worst as his second shot to the 11th flew unerringly towards a pond. As he anticipated hearing the dreaded splash to denote that his ball had indeed found a watery grave, the fates took a hand and instead the ball hit a rock on the edge of the water and bounced on to the green. In jubilation at his escape, Cruickshank threw his club into the air but made the basic mistake of then forgetting about its trajectory. As the club descended from the heavens, Cruickshank was still applauding his good fortune...until it made a crash landing on his head.

166 ON ONE HOLE

The jewel in the crown of abysmal golfers is the unnamed woman who, in the qualifying round of the Shawnee Invitational for Ladies at Shawnee-on-Delaware, Pennsylvania, took a cool 166 strokes for the 130 yard 16th hole. Her problems began when she drove her tee shot into the Binniekill River and the ball floated downstream. Not to be denied, this resourceful woman clambered into a boat with her husband at the oars and set off in pursuit of her ball. Eventually a mile and a half further down the river, her spouse keeping score, she succeeded in beaching the ball on terra firma. But there was more drama to come since the journey back to the 16th green necessitated playing through a wood. But when you've shot the Binniekill rapids in the course of a par 3, it takes more than a few trees to deter you. And so 165 shots and nearly two hours after driving off, she holed out. It is not known whether she qualified for the later stages of the tournament.

PROBABLY THE WORST MISTAKE IN THE WORLD

Competing in the Carlsberg Women's Professional Tournament at Wolverhampton back in June 1979, Suzanne Parker completed the outward nine in 45. Alas, when it came to filling in her card, she inadvertantly put that figure in the space reserved for her score on the 9th hole. Officials ruled that the score marked on the card had to stand and so her round rocketed to 121.

COOKED HIS GOOSE

Putting on the 17th at Congressional Country Club, a Dr. Sherman A. Thomas from Washington D.C. was half-way through his backswing when a Canadian goose, lurking nearby, honked loudly as if to suggest that the ball would miss to the left. Not surprisingly, the doctor did miss the putt – but not the goose. For in a fit of pique, he pursued the bird and felled it with a blow to the head (it is not recorded which club he selected for the task). Up before the local beak, he was fined $500 for killing a goose out of season, the Federal Magistrate giving short shrift to the medical man's rather limp claim that the goose had been wounded by his approach shot and that he was merely putting it out of its misery.

HARD TO PLEASE

Most golfers would be only too delighted to get a hole in one, but not 25-year-old Mark Law. For at the time Mark, who holed out at Goring and Streatley, Oxfordshire, was taking part in a long-driving competition! He sighed: 'It was just my luck to score a hole in one when I didn't want to.'

12-PUTTED

The 1968 French Open at St. Cloud was not a happy event for Britain's Brian Barnes. After three shots to the 8th, he was just three feet from the hole but, missing one putt, he then hurriedly attempted to hit a moving ball and also incurred a penalty for standing astride the line of a putt. The result was that a further 12 shots were added to his total and he took a calamitous 15 for the hole.

GEORGIA ON HIS MIND

Tom Weiskopf is unlikely ever to forget his experience on the inglorious 12th at Augusta, Georgia, home of the US Masters. Guarded to the front by a formidable stretch of water known as Rae's Creek, the 12th has been the graveyard of many a fine player and is said to be haunted by ghosts of the Indian burial ground that was disturbed when the green was under construction. Weiskopf fell victim to the Indian sign in 1980 when he hit five balls into the creek on his way to a nightmare 13. By the second round, he had got the hang of it and improved to a seven but still felt compelled to describe it as a 'hell hole'. Every month over 5,000 reservations are made to play the hole. Just one tee shot is allowed per person and they cannot take a second shot if the ball does not land on the green. Only one in 20 need their putter.

LANDED ON THE GREENS

A member of the John O'Gaunt Club at Sutton, near Biggleswade, was dismayed to produce just about the longest drive in history– one of some 42 miles. That was because he drifted just a little way out of bounds. To be precise, his ball landed in a passing vegetable lorry and finished up in London where it fell out of a box of cabbages being unloaded at Covent Garden. Rather than wait a few days for its possible return, it is believed he played a second ball.

HARDLY WORTH TURNING UP

P oor Mollie McBride might have been better off staying in bed than bothering to compete in the 1921 Canadian Ladies' Championship at Rivermead, Ottawa. For her opponent, Miss Cecil Leitch, was definitely not in a charitable frame of mind. Consequently, Mollie found herself 14 holes down at the end of the first round and after just three holes of the second round, she had succumbed to a crushing defeat by 17 and 15. Throughout the ordeal, she had held her own on just three occasions, halving two holes and actually winning the 9th. That at least was something for her to cherish.

NO JOKE

Comedian Tim Brooke-Taylor once took 12 shots to extricate himself from a bunker on the 17th at Effingham, Surrey, while partnering Tommy Horton in the Harry Secombe Golf Classic. Tim recalls: 'I know it was 12 because a spectator reminded me 15 years later. He claims the famous Hamlet cigar commercial was based on my performance because, so he says, a representative of the advertising agency was there.'

DOUG'S DISASTER

Few who witnessed it will ever forget the torment of America's Doug Sanders in the 1970 Open at St. Andrews. He had a putt of just three feet to win the Open which was even less than Bernard Langer's infamous Ryder Cup miss in 1991. Sanders set himself up for the putt but then bent forward to remove a wisp of grass. His nerve had clearly gone and the ball duly slipped by to the right. What's more, he went on to lose the play-off to Jack Nicklaus.

HAPLESS HARRY

American professional Harry Gonder was hell bent on achieving a hole in one. So one day in 1940, armed with two witnesses and a supply of caddies to tee up and retrieve balls, he embarked on an endurance test to see how long it would take him to achieve the magic ace on a 160-yard hole. For a golfer of his standing, he thought it would be a matter of half an hour or so, certainly no more than a couple of hours. Ball after ball he hit towards the flag. His 86th attempt finished just 15 inches short but other than that, he was having difficulty finding his range. As the hours ticked by, Harry started to feel hungry and after 941 balls, he stopped for refreshment in the hope that it would change his fortunes. It so nearly worked for his 996th hit the pin and bounced three inches away. On and on he went. At 8.10pm, his 1,162nd shot stopped six inches short and, beginning to get into his stride at last, his 1,184th missed by three inches. It was a false dawn. As the church bells struck midnight, Harry struck his 1,600th ball. Like most of its predecessors, it finished nowhere near the target. By now fatigue was beginning to set in and a nasty blister appeared on his hand. Still he battled on and was so nearly rewarded twice in the space of a few minutes. His 1,750th hit the pin as did the 1,756th which ended up just one measly inch from the hole. That seemed to convince Harry that even if he carried on into 1941, he was never going to get that elusive hole in one. At 2.40am, 16 hrs 25mins after he had first teed off, Harry's 1,817th shot finished ten long feet from the pin...and he gave up.

LEAST HOSPITABLE COURSE

A course to avoid at all costs is the one which opened in Kenya in the 1960s. One of the rules states that if your ball lands on or by a crocodile, you have the option of moving the ball a club's length away – or moving the crocodile.

THE MAN FROM DEL MONTE

Curiously in golf it is often a case of the shorter the hole, the bigger the headache. Take American Hans Merell who, on 17 January 1959 during the third round of the BingCrosby National Tournament at Del Monte, California, managed to take 19 to complete the 222-yard par-3 16th.

BIG BUILD-UP

The Australian PGA event was once started by a colourful individual who insisted on giving the golfers a Palladium-style introduction as they stood on the first tee. 'Next from Nationalist China,' he proclaimed, 'we have Cho Ling-Low. He doesn't swing the scales far, but my word, would you watch him hit this one.' Poor Mr. Cho, barely 5ft tall, was sadly unable to live up to his newly-acquired reputation as one of the game's big hitters. His drive bounced three times before trickling into the 200-yard cross bunkers.

ROUGH JUSTICE

The least successful ruling in the history of golf must be that which a US Open official tried to impose on Walter Hagen in the 1919 tournament. On the 17th hole of the play-off, Hagen had sliced into the rough and his ball ended up on a patch of extremely soft ground. It was found embedded in the mud amidst claims that it had been trodden on by members of the gallery. Nevertheless the official ruled that the ball should be played as it was. Hagen protested and asked to identify the ball. The official agreed and turned the ball over a number of times but still Hagen maintained that he was not convinced that it was his. By the time Hagen accepted the situation, most of the mud had been removed by the somewhat gullible official. The soil around was loose and the ball was once more playable .

UNLUCKY JIM

Surrey pub landlord Jim Meade expected stiff competition on his golfing society's day out. What he didn't expect was to land up in hospital after being knocked out twice in a matter of seconds by flying golf balls. Jim was minding his own business searching for his ball in the rough when from an adjoining fairway a ball hurtled through the trees, ricocheted off a branch and hit him between the eyes. As people rushed to Jim's aid and helped him to his feet, he was immediately struck again by another player's sliced drive. He ended up needing four stitches to his forehead and was left with a bump which appropriately was the size of a golf ball. Battered and bruised, Jim said: 'I can't believe this has happened to me. I thought I was in a war zone. I didn't know much about the first strike, but two of the lads were helping me to my feet when there was another shout of fore. They hit the deck, left me staggering about and the ball whacked me in the middle of the back. I stumbled, went down again and just flaked out. Now they want me to hold the flag on every hole so they can be sure of hitting the target!'

DOWN TO EARTH

The experiences of Tommy Armour in 1927 amply illustrate the ups and downs of golf. Just a week after winning the US Open, Armour was playing in the Shawnee Open. But any hopes he had of repeating his triumph were shattered at the 17th at which he took 23 strokes, hooking a succession of balls out of bounds.

SEX CHANGE

About to tee off at the start of the Glen Campbell Los Angeles open, Clive Clark stepped forward to hear the starter proclaim: 'And next on the tee from London, England, we have Olive Clark.'

ONE MAN WENT TO MOW

Many people remarked about the length of the grass on the Lindrick greens for the first day of the 1957 Ryder Cup. The reason was simple – the greenkeeper at the Yorkshire club thought the competition was starting a day later than it was. In the circumstances, I suppose the United States and Great Britain teams were lucky they didn't have to wave through a ladies' foursomes.

COOK ROASTED

Eight holes up with just eight to play at the Army Golf Club, Aldershot, on 5 July 1974, Mike Cook already had one hand on the coveted Gradoville Bowl. Then in the manner of all great sporting failures, he fell apart completely, allowing his opponent, M.C. Smart, to win every remaining hole. By now thoroughly dejected, Cook also threw in the first play-off hole for good measure.

HOLE IN ONE

Driving off the first tee at Blackmoor Golf Club at Bordon, Hampshire, a player was amazed to see his ball disappear down the hole. Unfortunately, it was the hole of a chimney 120 yards away and 40 yards out of bounds on the right. It also came as quite a surprise to the owner of the house and his wife who were sitting in front of the fire at the time.

SECOND-CLASS MALE

In the 1950s, one Colonel H. Nugent-Head, a noted long hitter and it would seem something of a chauvinist, proudly boasted that no woman could beat him on any course playing level. He found a filly that was prepared to take him on, a lady by the name of Frances Stephens, and no doubt to a crescendo of cheers from lady golfers, she beat him 3 and 2.

SUPERGRASS

British golfer Jamie Spence left the third round of the 1993 Rome Masters as joint-leader and on the way to the chance of a £50,000 payout. But his hopes were dashed by an eagle-eyed spectator who had seen Spence mistakenly drop in the wrong place off a path and had felt it his duty to tell an official. Four hours after his round had been completed, the luckless Spence was hauled back to the course to undergo trial by television. Having watched the action replay, the organizers disqualified him for signing for a score which did not include a two-stroke penalty.

JUST TOO LATE

*B*rigadier-General Critchley had set his heart on competing in the 1937 Amateur Championship at Sandwich. And to prove it he was travelling all the way from New York to take part. Unfortunately, his Atlantic crossing on the Queen Mary was delayed by fog and the ship was therefore late docking at Southampton. However the military man was nothing if not well-prepared and had taken the precaution of hiring an aeroplane to take him to Sandwich. Realizing he was cutting it fine as he reached the Kent coast, he circled over the clubhouse so that officials knew his arrival would be imminent. But in golf, rules are rules and there is no room for sentiment. The Brigadier-General did make it to the clubhouse but he was a whole six minutes late and his name had been irrevocably struck out. At the same championship, an entrant from Burma who had travelled across the Pacific and the American continent, also had the misfortune to be on board the fog-bound Queen Mary. He lacked the far-sightedness of Brigadier-General Critchley and travelled from Southampton to Sandwich by car, eventually arriving four hours after his allocated starting time. Despite having trekked half-way around the world, he too was struck out. It must have been a long journey home.

POLITICAL APOLOGY

*F*ormer US Vice President Spiro Agnew was at his most dangerous with a golf club in his hand. His hook was deadlier than Henry Cooper's. It was because organizers knew that there would never be a dull moment, nor a spectator standing, when Agnew was around that he became much in demand for celebrity tournaments. Agnew didn't mind who he hit – professional golfers and ordinary members of the public came alike to him. Once at the Bob Hope Classic, one of his trademark wayward shots struck Doug Sanders on the head. Rushing out a letter of apology (it was rumoured he had them ready-printed), he also sent Sanders a memento of the occasion in the form of a silver tray on which was engraved in large letters the word 'FORE'.

JACK'S OFF DAY

Just to prove that even the mighty are human, Jack Nicklaus shot an inspired 83 in the first round of the 1981 Open at Royal St. George's, Sandwich. And he only achieved that by completing the last four holes in level par. He had four double-bogeys and his piece de resistance, giving hope to millions, was a tee shot on the par-5 14th which travelled no further than 80 yards. After what was at the time his worst-ever round as a professional golfer, the usually co-operative Nicklaus declined to give any press interviews for fear that he might say something he would later regret. His score sent shock waves around the world of golf and on the television news that night, it was mentioned even before that of the leader.

FALSE ALARM

The Point Grey Golf and Country Club in Vancouver, British Columbia, reacted swiftly to news that a golfer had suffered a heart attack out on the course. They immediately notified the emergency services and sure enough within minutes an ambulance crew was on the scene to tend to the patient. But as it turned out, they need not have hurried. The alarm had been raised after a passing golfer had noticed 95-year-old Justice J.M. Coody, a retired member of British Columbia's Supreme Court, resting in a golf buggy. The man asked what the problem was and he thought the judge replied, 'Heart failure'. He hadn't. In fact,

*the only likely demise was that of Justice Coody's buggy
which had stalled. And what he had actually said was,
'Cart failure'.*

BUNKERED!

Amateur golfer Melville Bucher was thoroughly
enjoying playing with the big boys in the 1955 Open
at St. Andrews. He had survived the cut and made it
through to the final round where, whilst not exactly
threatening the leader board, he was going along
merrily enough. Until the par-3 11th that is. For there
he put his tee shot into the awkward Strath bunker. At
one point Mr. Bucher must have thought he was going
to be like Hitler and never get out of the bunker but
finally six shots later he emerged. However, he finished
up taking ten for the hole and ruined an otherwise
respectable round.

OH DEER

*A natural hazard of playing Wollaton Park Golf Club in
Nottingham is the herd of red deer that wanders the
course. Most of the year they sit quietly in the rough or
under trees but come the rutting season they are a different
proposition altogether. So when two golfers strolled around
the course blissfully unaware of the deer calendar, they
thought nothing of the fact that their shots had landed right
next to a huge stag. And they didn't think much of it when
the stag, which seemed to be carrying a full set of clubs on
its head, menacingly chased them towards the green. Wisely
they decided to abandon a lost cause and agreed on a free
drop the other side of the fairway.*

MID-AIR COLLISION

During the 1980 Corfu International Championship, Sharon Peachey saw her drive collide in mid-air with a ball from a competitor playing a different hole. Not only did Sharon lose vital yardage but her ball finished up in a pond!

DEVLIN'S DIP

Coming to the 18th in the 1975 San Diego Open at Torrey Pines, Australia's Bruce Devlin was right up there in the prize money. But that hole was to prove a blow to his pride and to his wallet. For, having landed in a shallow pond, Devlin made the mistake of thinking that he could somehow play his way out. He waded in and, wielding his club, started to splash around frantically without ever making much contact with the ball. When all hope seemed lost, he did eventually emerge – but it was six shots later. And the 10 he took for the 18th cost him $3,000. Course officials were so taken by Devlin's single-minded determination flying in the face of common sense that they decided to erect a plaque at the scene of the mayhem, christening it 'Devlin's Pond'. To his credit, Devlin himself saw the amusing side but suggested Australianizing it to 'Devlin's Billabong'.

BLIND DATE

Former US Open Champion J.J. McDermott must have forgotten to look at his diary before travelling to Britain to compete in the qualifying rounds for the 1914 Open at Prestwick. For he got the wrong week and having journeyed across the Atlantic, he arrived on the very day that qualifying finished.

CRUEL LUCK

Competing in the prestigious Tournament Players Championship at Sydney in 1989, Australia's Bob Emond enjoyed the sort of excursions on a par-5 normally reserved for the humblest Sunday morning golfer. Once he had landed in the water for the fourth time, he knew it was going to be one of those holes. Thoroughly miserable, he made matters worse by allowing one of his penalty drops to hit his shoe, thereby incurring a further two-stroke loss. By now he had taken 11 and was still nowhere near the green. Manfully he struggled on, only to suffer a further self-inflicted wound when collecting another two-stroke penalty (his 15th and 16th shots) for marking a ball that was not on the green. Finally, he three putted for a 19. His reaction was unprintable.

A FAIR COP

Just about the unluckiest burglars in the annals of crime were the pair who in 1989 decided to rob a house bordering Warley Park Golf Club in Essex. They were caught in the act by no fewer than 24 off-duty policemen out on a golf day!

SOAKED TO THE SKIN

Surely the least successful autograph hunters in the world were those who surrounded Gary Player in 1976 as he came off the 18th green at the Congressional Country Club following a practice round. Such was the clamour for the South African's signature that in the ensuing scrimmage the boys accidentally pushed him in a lake!

IT'S A KNOCKOUT

Selecting a wood to drive off the 17th tee at Lyme Regis, Dorset, 69-year-old Derek Gatley was half-way through his backswing when the steel shaft snapped and the club struck him on the back of the head, knocking him out. When he came to, Mr Gatley admitted: 'It was the first thing I had hit all day!'

PROFESSIONAL HIT-MAN

As he stood on the 18th tee at St. Margaret's-at-Cliffe in Kent, club professional W.J. Robinson was supremely confident of clearing the cow which was grazing 100 yards up the fairway. But this bovine hazard proved more than a match for Robinson whose drive clattered into the unsuspecting creature. Sadly the cow was killed, leaving Robinson with what can only be described as an awkward second shot.

HERMAN MONSTER

Troon's famous 126-yard 8th, otherwise known as the Postage Stamp because of its miniscule green, has destroyed many a reputation. And it didn't do much for the prospects of German amateur Herman Tissies who, competing in the first qualifying round for the 1950 Open, took a monstrous 15. Having missed the green with his tee-shot, Herr Tissies proceeded to spend several minutes zig-zagging across the sward from bunker to bunker, presumably in search of one he liked. Finally, he managed to stop his 14th stroke on the green. Just when it seemed that spectators would be in for another treat watching the German attempt to hole out, he spoiled their fun by one-putting.

RUGBY UNION

LOST HIS BEARINGS

Brunei rugby player Dick Dover was nothing if not keen. So when, playing for Kukris against Panaga, he saw the opportunity to break with the ball from a scrum, he set off on a memorable 75-yard run to touch down unchallenged. He leaped to his feet in anticipation of hearty congratulations from his team-mates but was surprised to see that they appeared to be more puzzled than pleased. That was because not-so-clever Dick had been disorientated by the wheeling of the scrum and had run the 75 yards to 'score' near his own posts...

FRENCH BREAD

Gaston Vareilles was honoured to be selected to play for France against Scotland in 1911 and enjoyed the camaraderie of travelling to the match by train with his new international colleagues. But the butterflies in his stomach left him feeling a little empty so when the train stopped at a station, he decided to jump off and buy a sandwich. However, he had failed to anticipate the possibility of a queue and returned to the platform to see the train and his team-mates disappearing into the distance. He missed the match and, apparently to his surprise, was never picked for France again.

INJURED BY HIS CAPTAIN

When the British Lions toured South Africa, skipper Willie John McBride used a novel, and sometimes painful, method of geeing up his team before a big game. He would line all the players up in the dressing room and, working his way along, would thump each man in the chest, at the same time calling out their name. The idea was that it would create a sense of purpose and unity. The ritual was duly performed prior to the Third Test but on this occasion for some reason McBride decided to hit Scotland's Gordon Brown twice. Brown had been expecting the first blow but not the second and was so badly winded that the kick-off had to be delayed while he received attention. The incident may well have broken new ground as being the first instance of a sponge man having to leave the field to go into the dressing room to treat a player before the match had even started.

TROUBLE BREWING

Devotees of humiliating defeats were cheated of a possible record in this department when the spoilsport of a referee abandoned Corby's Northern tour match at Whitby in 1989. At the time, just seven minutes of the second half had been played and Corby were already losing 80–0. The referee's decision was based upon the fact that he considered several of the Corby players were too drunk to continue. One Corby man admitted: 'We did sink a few last night.' At which point he fell over.

DANISH DISASTER

Even a totally paralytic side would have been hard pushed to equal the achievement of Danish club Lindo in 1973. These Danes were far from great as they were crushed 194–0 by a team called Comet.

MEDAL MEDDLING

The least successful attempt to decide the rightful winners of an Olympic gold medal must surely rest with the organizers of the 1920 Antwerp games. Even to this day, both France and the United States claim that they won the rugby union gold. Although staged in Belgium, the Antwerp Olympics were naturally run by the French and organized by Baron de Coubertin. France insist that the gold should be theirs by virtue of their 14–5 victory over the US at Stade Colombes on 10 October 1920. But the Americans say that match didn't count and they point to their 8–0 win against the French in Antwerp three months earlier. France dismiss that encounter, maintaining that it was a game of American Football. And anyway, they say, the kindly Baron only agreed to send a group of players to Antwerp in the first place out of the goodness of his heart and to uphold the Olympic spirit. There's plenty more years left in this one yet.

BLIND SIDE FORWARD

The 1993 Coal Board Cup tie between Nottinghamshire's Silverhill Colliery and Daw Mill from Warwickshire was held up for several minutes while players searched for a team-mate's glass eye. It belonged to 14-stone Silverhill forward Steve Bush who lost the sight of his left eye in an underground pit accident three years previously. But the search was in vain and Steve had to play the rest of the match with an empty eye socket. Although this must have been a somewhat disconcerting sight to the opposition, Silverhill still lost 17–8. Mick said: 'We had just gone down for a scrum and I was giving it a good shove. The lads reckon I was putting in so much effort that it made my eyes go pop.' Referee Peter Llewellyn added: 'I saw this player walking round staring at the ground. I asked, "What have you lost?" When he said "My eye" I thought we had a major injury on our hands.'

LACK OF COURAGE

Playing in Division Three of the Durham/Northumberland Courage Clubs Championship, Hartlepool Athletic were pipped 146–0 when they visited Billingham on 3 October 1987. A Hartlepool official confessed: 'We never really looked like winning.'

DYEING TO PLAY

There looked to be little prospect of play in the 1935 international between Uganda and Kenya at Entebbe when both teams took to the field in white shirts. While the referee pondered on the impracticality of the situation, a lady spectator suddenly raced on to the pitch carrying a vast bottle of black dye, an item which was clearly part of her everyday baggage. While all around her looked on in amazement, this resourceful individual promptly set about dyeing the home side's shirts. There was no time to allow them to dry and so with their newly-coloured kit still wet, the Ugandans played the match in black.

HISTORY REPEATING ITSELF

Supreme confidence could be said to be a national characteristic of Americans. Thus in the Hong Kong Sevens one year, the US coach had absolutely no doubts whatsoever that his team would wipe the floor with Japan. Defeat, along with quite a few other things like tactics, had never entered his head. For a start, his boys were huge whereas the Japanese were so tiny it was almost laughable. So with great expectations, he settled to watch the US kick off. The ball sailed into the air, was caught by a Japanese player and a few lightning passes later was touched down for a try beneath the American posts. With their invincibility still not open to question, the Americans tried the same thing again...with the same result. And for a third time so that after barely three minutes' play, the US were trailing 18–0. It was too much for their coach to bear. He sank to his knees and yelled to anyone who was listening: 'Pearl Harbour I can forgive, but not this!'

EARLY START

It is a wonder Fiji bothered playing any internationals after the experience of their very first overseas trip to Western Samoa in 1924. The tourists were forced to pay all their own fares and the match had to be played at the unearthly hour of 7am in order to allow the Samoans to go off to work afterwards. Just to round things off, the stadium at Apia was notable for having a large tree in the centre of the pitch which presumably made kicking-off rather a problem.

SICK LEAVE

On the morning of a France versus Scotland international in Paris, a London Scottish XV had a match arranged against a local junior side. The previous night, a number of the visiting players had been partaking of the grape and were consequently feeling a shade delicate come kick-off. Nevertheless, their prowess carried them through unscathed until ten minutes from time when their loosehead was suddenly sick all over the ball at a scrum. Until that point, London Scottish had won every single scrum but when this one also appeared about to go their way, their hooker, observing the vomit-encrusted object, decided to leave it

and struck the ball back through the ruck of players. That
solitary scrum went to the home team, at which the visitors'
number eight called out: 'Good ball to lose, Scottish!'

SNAKE CHARM

When the first Australian rugby union tourists came to
Britain in 1908, their mascot was a live snake. It
brought them plenty of good fortune and they remained
unbeaten. But then the snake's luck ran out – it died.
And with it went the Australians' record for they
immediately lost their next game at Llanelli.

DISGRACEFUL SCENES

Drunken rugby players were escorted from a jet after they
brawled, sang bawdy songs, told rude jokes and bared their
bottoms on a flight from Canada to London. Police met the

plane at Gatwick airport but were taken aback to discover that the rowdy players from Brampton Rugby Club in Toronto were all women.

BEATEN 200–0

Scores of over 100 in rugby union are pretty rare although there have been a few in internationals. Among the sufferers were Nigeria who lost 111–12 to Zimbabwe at Nairobi in 1987; and in 1988 Paraguay crashed 106–12 to France in Asuncion. But these are close-fought encounters compared to the English Schools' match of 20 November 1886 in which Hills Court went down 200–0 to Radford.

SOME FRIENDLY!

Right from the kick-off, a so-called 'friendly' rugby union match between Bramley and West Park Bramhope in March 1991 was marred by constant niggling among the players. Steadily, this escalated into a series of ugly brawls which culminated in referee Terry Cork abandoning the match because of persistent foul play. West Park led 4–0 at the time. All 30 players were later suspended for several weeks.

INJURED BEFORE START

About to take the field for the 1969 international with Scotland in Paris, Frenchman Jean-Pierre Salut tripped as he was running up the stairs from the dressing room to the pitch and broke his ankle. He was thus carried off before he had even made it onto the pitch.

TEETHING TROUBLES

*O*n 21 July 1964, South Africa decided to stage their international with France away from their usual venues at Johannesburg or Cape Town. Instead they chose the Pam Brink Stadium at Springs, but the exercise was an unmitigated disaster. A crowd of 25,000 was admitted, far more than the ground could comfortably accommodate, with the result that hardly anybody was able to see the match properly. In protest, the crowd kept the ball whenever it was kicked into touch. With so many replacement balls being used, it proved an expensive match for the authorities whose mood was not lightened by the fact that South Africa lost 8–6. To cap it all, after the match there was a fire in the car park.

HUSBAND, WIFE AND DOG SENT OFF

A s a consequence of what can only be construed as some domestic dispute, Mrs. Christine Kenyon marched on to the pitch during the 1989 fixture between Aretians Thirds and Bristol Saracens to remonstrate bitterly with one of the players, her husband Mike. Receiving no satisfaction, she deposited his kit bag and pet dog at his feet. While the other players looked on in wonderment, the referee decided to take firmer action and ordered the two humans and one canine to the touch line. One spectator said of Mrs. Kenyon's interruption: 'These days it's not often you get a woman invading the pitch with her clothes on.'

AN ESSENTIAL INGREDIENT

*I*n 1966 Colwyn Bay RFC set off on their 50-mile journey to play Welsh rivals Portmadoc. Once there, they got changed, the referee ran out onto the pitch and both teams were lined up ready for the kick-off when it was suddenly realized that something was missing – there was no ball. So the match was abandoned.

RUGBY LEAGUE

<u>WORST RUGBY LEAGUE TEAM</u>

This honour undoubtedly belongs to Runcorn Highfield who lost 61 Cup and League matches in a row from January 1989 to February 1991. Their actual record without a win was even more dismal, stretching to 75 games between October 1988 and March 1991, and in season 1989–90 they lost all 28 League fixtures. So few among the mighty crowd of 300 who were packed into Hoghton Road on 3 February 1991 will forget the scenes of jubilation as Runcorn finally stopped the rot by holding visiting Carlisle to a 12–12 draw. Inspired by the fact that they had actually not lost a match (a sensation which many of their players had never experienced before), Runcorn went on to achieve that elusive victory a month later when Dewsbury were beaten 9–2. Hooker Geoff Dean, who was young enough to have played in Runcorn's previous win against Fulham on 30 October 1988, said: 'It's difficult to describe how happy we all felt.' Runcorn's fortunes were arguably at their lowest ebb in 1989 on the day they went out of the JPS Trophy 92–2 at the hands of Wigan. Runcorn were forced to field nine amateurs because their players had gone on strike (rumour had it that the dispute was over win bonuses...) Consequently their coach, Bill Ashurst, a 41-year-old born-again Christian, was named as one of the substitutes. He came on in the second half but 11 minutes later was sent off for head-butting!

SLIPPED DISC

Thirty-two cardboard discs were placed in the bag ready for the draw for the first round of the 1923–24 Rugby League Challenge Cup. But mysteriously Hunslet's disc became stuck to the bottom of Swinton's and when the draw was apparently completed, everyone suddenly realized that one disc was missing. So poor old Hunslet were given the remaining space which, being the last position in the draw, was an away game, against Salford. Hunslet vehemently protested but it was to no avail, the League insisting that the draw had to stand.

MASTER PLAN

Few managers can have played such an important part in their team's preparations for a big match as did Salford manager Lance Todd in the lead-up to the 1939 Challenge Cup Final with Halifax. In the week before the final, Todd hit upon the idea of taking his team out training in the wilds of the countryside. Alas, the barn which he had hired for the players to use as training accommodation didn't have any baths. As a result most of the team caught colds and they still had them when they walked out at Wembley. Tired and weak, Salford's noses ran faster than their legs. They flopped 20–3 which, considering they were hot pre-match favourites, just shows what a stroke of genius it was by Todd.

RAIL CHAOS

Such was the excitement engendered by the 1910 Challenge Cup Final between Hull and Leeds that a flotilla of special trains was laid on to take spectators to the venue at

Huddersfield. Five trains were laid on from Leeds and 14 from far-flung Hull. Anyone who has ever been on a rail excursion will not be in the least surprised to learn that neither team made it to the final in time, necessitating the kick-off to be put back until 4.20pm. Hull set off at noon but it took them two hours to get from Leeds to Huddersfield by train. Indeed they had even seen the Leeds team on the platform waiting for their train to the match. Fittingly, the game ended in stalemate at 7–7 with Leeds going on to win the replay.

OFFIAH PUT OUT

Great Britain's record-breaking winger Martin Offiah suffered a rare but costly lapse in the Third Test against New Zealand at Christchurch in July 1990 . The game was only three minutes old when Offiah was left with a simple opportunity to finish a brilliant 75-yard team move. But attempting to make a one-handed touchdown between the posts, he succeeded in losing the ball. Although he did score five minutes from time, his mistake sent Great Britain stumbling to a 21–18 defeat. While the habitual match-winner sat silently in the dressing room afterwards, one commentator remarked bluntly: 'Offiah's blunder would have shamed a schoolboy.'

WIRES CROSSED

One of the least successful radio broadcasts was that made at the 1928 Challenge Cup Final between Swinton and Warrington when listeners back in Warrington were given the distinct impression that their team's scrum half, Billy Kirk, was dead. Kirk had been badly injured during the game and when two people ran on to the field to attend to him, it was assumed that they were clergymen, possibly because their collars were reversed. Kirk was lifted on to a stretcher, covered completely and removed from the pitch. Many people present thought he was dead and the radio broadcasters fuelled that belief back in his home town. In fact, Kirk recovered and went on to live for a good number of years.

CITY SLACKERS

Liverpool City only lasted one season in the League, 1906–7, which, in view of their record during their brief sojourn, was probably just as well. They lost all 30 of their League matches plus the two Cup ties they played. They did actually manage a home League draw against Bramley but when they were unable to fulfil the return fixture, the match was expunged from League records. All in all, they weren't a great loss to the city's sporting heritage.

THE MAN FROM NOWHERE

A third-round Challenge Cup tie between Swinton and Castleford in 1927–28 was evenly balanced when Castleford launched a breakaway attack which looked certain to produce a try. With the Swinton defence in disarray, Castleford headed for the line, only to be denied by a try-saving tackle from someone who hadn't even been on the pitch. It was made by an injured Swinton player who had been off the field receiving treatment. Seeing the breakaway, he suddenly reappeared on the scene and launched himself at the unsuspecting Castleford man. To make matters worse, Castleford went on to lose but the incident did lead to a change in the rules to ensure that there was no repetition of such dark deeds. Certainly had it not been checked, it could have set dangerous precedents whereby visiting wingers would set off for the corner with the constant fear that any minute they were likely to be bundled into touch by three programme-sellers, a steward and a hot dog salesman.

BIG MATCH NERVES

The 1933 Challenge Cup Final between Warrington and Huddersfield was set to be a particularly poignant occasion with the promise of the first attendance by a member of the Royal family. Unfortunately, King George V failed a late fitness test because of a nagging cold so it was Edward Prince of Wales who deputized at Wembley. The pomp and ceremony was all too much for Warrington stand-off half Jack Oster who was so tense before kick-off that his team-mates virtually had to carry him on to the pitch. Nor did his nerves subside once the game was under way and he made the error which resulted in Huddersfield's match-winning try.

DIRE DONS

*A*lthough not quite in the same class as Runcorn Highfield, Doncaster did manage to lose 40 consecutive League games between 16 November 1975 and 21 April 1977. Who knows, with a little more practice, they could well have extended their sequence and presented an even more formidable target.

FOX COUNTS HIS CHICKENS

*E*ven today, the 1968 Challenge Cup Final is remembered for Don Fox's dramatic failure with the last kick of the game. On a rain-soaked pitch, Wakefield Trinity and Leeds had been locked in an energy-sapping battle. Leeds held the upper hand until in the last minute, Wakefield's Ken Hirst splashed over for a sensational try to cut Leeds' advantage to 11–10. Leeds thought it was all over for them since Fox, who had already kicked two penalties, was left with a simple kick in front of the posts to win the Cup for Wakefield. The Leeds players couldn't bear to watch but as Fox stepped up to kick what seemed a formality, his standing foot slipped on the wet turf and the ball squirted to the right of the posts. Leeds couldn't believe it. One player said: 'When he missed, it took a few seconds before we realized what had happened.' Fox still won the Lance Todd Trophy as man of the match which, in view of Mr. Todd's achievement back in 1939, was considered by some to be quite appropriate.

FANS MISSED FIRST HALF

*T*he very first Challenge Cup Final, between Batley and St. Helens on 24 April 1897, should have been a day to remember for players and fans alike. But for the St. Helens supporters, it was a day to forget since the vast majority of them missed virtually the entire first half. From the outset,

Saints had been unhappy about the choice of Headingley as
the venue for the final since it was an awkward train
journey to Leeds for their fans. Inevitably, the train carrying
the bulk of their supporters was delayed so that by the time
they arrived with the half-time whistle approaching, their
team was already heading for defeat. Things didn't improve
in the second half either and Saints finished up losing 10–3.
The game also sounded a note of warning to youngsters who
were in the habit of watching matches at Headingley from a
nearby tree. Batley's opening score, a drop goal from Joe
Oakland, was greeted with such raucous enthusiasm by the
crowd that the shock sent the two boys tumbling from their
lofty vantage point to the ground.

WHIPPING BOYS

Carlisle are one of the Cinderella clubs in Rugby League
and there were a couple of occasions in the 1980s
when they were definitely late for the ball. On 20
October 1984 a representative team from the area played
Humberside in the second round of the National Inter-
League Competition...and lost 138–0. Two years later
Carlisle faced St. Helens in the Lancashire Cup and were
on the receiving end of a 112–0 hiding. One of the first
great Rugby League massacres occurred on 28 February
1914 when Swinton Park Rangers were annihilated
119–2 by Huddersfield in the first round of the Northern
Union Cup. So abject were Swinton that they allowed
Huddersfield to run in no fewer than 27 tries.

STAND-OFFISH

Twenty-six-year-old stand-off Jamie Kahakura was a
popular newcomer with New Zealand club Whakaki. His
team-mates liked him although they did wonder why he

always avoided leaping in the bath with them afterwards. Then after playing in the Gisborne-East Coast Competition in 1989, the reason for Jamie's prudishness was revealed – and he was banned from playing for being female.

PRE-MATCH BLUNDER

The St. Helens Challenge Cup Final team of 1930 were presented with a hectic pre-match schedule which drained so much of their energy that they had precious little left for the match itself. For some reason, they journeyed everywhere in London on foot and so an evening training session at Wembley on the Thursday followed by a late-night visit to the town's MP at the House of Commons (no doubt the players really enjoyed that) wasn't exactly the ideal preparation for the game . No wonder when it came to the Saturday, they lost 10–3 to Widnes.

MYSTERY TOUR

The coach drive to Wembley offers players one last chance to sit back and relax before the big occasion – unless, that is, they were on board the Bradford Northern team bus bound for the 1947 Challenge Cup Final. The players and officials were sitting back taking in the sights when it slowly began to dawn on them that it was getting nearer and nearer to kick-off time yet there was still no sign of the Twin Towers. The driver tried to make a few reassuring noises but it soon became apparent that he was hopelessly lost. Luckily, help was at hand in the shape of prop forward Frank Whitcombe who happened to be the holder of an HGV licence. Thus the hapless driver was obliged to relinquish the wheel to allow Whitcombe to drive his team-mates safely to Wembley.

HORSE RACING

SHURE SHOT

In a pre-war race at the now defunct Hurst Park course just outside London, an old chaser called Nincompoop fell badly at the third last fence. The horse lay on the ground as if mortally wounded and the vet was duly summoned from the hospitality suite. He was told that the groundsman was comforting the horse which would need to be put down humanely. No doubt fuelled by an excess of port, the vet shakily raised his gun to perform the final deed and promptly shot the groundsman through the foot. At this point, the alarmed horse got to its feet and happily trotted off to the stables. And it went on to win 11 more races.

WAS IT PERSONAL?

Jump jockey Ron Atkins could be forgiven for thinking that a horse he once rode in a novice chase at Ascot harboured something of a grudge against him. First of all, the beast decided that it was happier jumping the fences without Atkins on its back and deposited him on the floor half-way round. Unhurt, the rider hitched a lift back in the course car and was dropped off near the finish once the race had come to its conclusion. But as he walked along the track towards the weighing room, Atkins was knocked unconscious by a loose horse – the very one which he had been riding in the race.

ALLERGIC TO WINNING

Amrullah is racing's most consistent horse – that is, he is consistently bad. By the autumn of 1992, he had raced (if that's not too strong a word for it) 74 times without winning once. Indeed he has rarely threatened to do so. Yet although retirement would have longed seemed the obvious option (some might suggest since he was a two-year-old), the 13-year-old gelding has become a favourite with the British public. We simply love a good loser and losers don't come any better than Amrullah. His trainer John Bridger revealed: 'We couldn't retire him because I kept getting so many calls from people wondering whether he was going to continue in racing. Besides he still seemed to love the idea of carrying on.'

SHORT MEASURES

Due to shortage of space, Leopardstown used to have a round five-furlong course but it was extremely unpopular with just about everyone since the horses were always on a bend. Eventually pressure forced Captain George Quin, who ran the course, to install a straight five-furlong track although he was still cramped for room. Aware that there was no official measuring of courses, Quin simply put down a start and a finish and proclaimed the distance between the two to be five furlongs. The track produced no end of shock results with many a horse simply being taken off its feet by the lightning pace. Then in 1897 trainer F.F. McCabe noted that his horse Sabine Queen was 10½ seconds faster at Leopardstown than over a five-furlong time trial at home. McCabe realized that there was only one possible reason for this difference and sure enough when the authorities were persuaded to measure the Leopardstown sprint track, they found that it was less than four and a half furlongs. Quin was fined £100 and the track was temporarily closed, pending construction of a proper five furlong track.

NATIONAL DISASTER

There is no need to scan the sporting pages of the last two centuries to unearth one of horse racing's greatest failures, certainly the one seen by the largest audience. It was the 1993 Grand National. It was to have been a proud day for 64-year-old starter, Captain Keith Brown, officiating at his last National. But his problems began when Animal Rights protesters gathered at the first fence, delaying the start by over ten minutes. When the 39 runners did come into line, the starting tape went up too slowly and caught under the horses' hooves. Captain Brown flourished his red flag to indicate a false start and recall man Ken Evans, stationed 100 yards further up the track, raced out to wave his red flag and send the runners back. By now, horses and jockeys were getting restless and when Captain Brown let them go for a second time, again the tape failed to rise properly, half-strangling jockey Richard Dunwoody on board Won't Be Gone Long. The horse couldn't have been more aptly named – he was unable to go anywhere. Eight others pulled up at the start but the rest of the field continued unchecked. The recall man hadn't seen the Captain's flag which this time was said to be tightly furled. On and on they went. There was an attempt to intercept at The Chair but the jockeys thought the officials running on the course with traffic cones were simply more protestors. Some riders pulled up at half-way but others pressed on. At the end of the two circuits, Jenny Pitman's 50-1 outsider Esha Ness was first past the post. But this was the Grand National that never was and the race was swiftly declared void. Esha Ness's jockey, John White, was suitably distraught. 'It wasn't until I saw fellow jockey Dean Gallagher standing on the ground past the finish and he shouted that there had been a false start, that I realised anything was wrong.' As recriminations continued, John Upson, trainer of the second favourite Zeta's Lad, fumed: 'It's an absolute disgrace that the world's number one race should be run like this. It could not happen in a point-to-point in Ireland.' His remark, although certainly not intended as criticism of Irish racing, unfortunately upset some Irish racegoers. When the dust eventually settled, the chief culprit in the 1993 Grand National was found to be the slack elastic of the starting tape. A Jockey Club spokesman ruled out vastly different starting methods. 'We have tried red and green lights, but they didn't show up in bright sunlight – and a klaxon just frightened the horses.'

BORN LOSER

In the wake of the Grand National, a man from Cornwall lamented to the *Daily Mirror*: 'I have done the pools for 28 years and never won a thing. My wife and I have held £213 in Premium Bonds since 1971 and not collected as much as a fiver. We have entered every draw, raffle and free competition available. Not a sausage! In the National I had a fiver on Esha Ness at 66–1. Do you think I am just unlucky?'

MILES OFF COURSE

Clearly a keen student of the Mark Thatcher road atlas, Midlands trainer Sally Oliver had a sad experience one day at Bangor. The stewards held an inquiry after one of Mrs. Oliver's horses had won at the tiny Shropshire course of Bangor-on-Dee. But a public address announcement failed to produce any sign of the trainer. It emerged that, having never been to Bangor before, she had consulted her map and headed for the other town of the same name, situated some 100 miles away on the North Wales coast!

EXPENSIVE FLOP

*S*heikh Mohammed forked out $10.2 million for Snaafi
*Dancer at the Keeneland Sales in Kentucky but the horse
proved so abysmal that it never even got on to a racecourse.*

HEROIC IN DEFEAT

By their very nature, novice chases are invariably hair-raising
affairs. And such an event at Newton Abbot on 28 August
1984 will live long in the memory of Mr. Stuart Kittow. He
was riding a horse called Tango Shandy. As the rest of the
field obligingly decided to dispense with the services of their
jockeys during the course of the race, only Tango Shandy and
Legal Session remained standing. And when Legal Session too
fell some way out, the result looked a foregone conclusion.
But as Mr Kittow and Tango Shandy approached the last in
splendid isolation, the saddle slipped. The horse made a
terrible mistake and very nearly fell. At this stage, the rider
also lost his irons but, determined to keep the partnership
intact up the run-in, he managed to hang on grimly around
the horse's neck. With no saddle at all now, Mr. Kittow
bounced along precariously towards the winning post until,
no more than a few yards from the line, tragedy struck and he
slipped and hit the ground. Still this gallant individual would
not be denied and he desperately clung to the reins as he was
dragged across the finishing line. As far as he was concerned,
Mr. Kittow had won the race since he still had some form of
contact, albeit tenuous, with the horse when it passed the
post. Indeed the judge, possibly out of sympathy, awarded him
the race but sadly the stewards took a different view and
disqualified horse and rider. Instead the spoils went to Legal
Session who had remounted to finish a distant second, a short
while before the next race was due off. Deprived of victory,
Mr. Kittow had the satisfaction of being heartily cheered to
the unsaddling enclosure (a superfluous requirement in this
case) by the appreciative crowd.

ONLY FOOLS AND HORSES

The second favourite for the 1952 Goodwood Cup was a useful horse called Aquino II. It had been backed down to 2/1 but the day of the race was extremely hot and the horse simply did not fancy racing. As soon as they were off in the long-distance event, Aquino tried to turn round and head back to the paddock. Frustrated in that manoeuvre, it ran on for a furlong and then swerved violently out from the rails into the middle of the course and did its utmost to pull up. The jockey cajoled Aquino into some from of forward momentum until, reaching the bend out of the straight, the horse spotted from behind its blinkers an adjacent field of long grass, speckled with purple wild flowers. This looked the place to be on a nice sunny day and when a gap in the railings soon appeared, Aquino II calmly ambled off the course and into the field where it grazed happily, watching the other runners complete the remaining two miles.

MISDIRECTED

Approaching the second last in a conditional jockeys' chase at Uttoxeter in October 1992, Gold Haven and the Queen Mother's Norman Conqueror were suddenly directed around the fence by a bystander who thought an injured jockey was lying on the other side. He was wrong. And although Gold Haven got up to beat the Royal horse in a tight finish, the drama had only just begun because both horses were then disqualified for not jumping the second last. The race was awarded to third-placed Sam Shorrock.

DEAD CERT

A Canadian bought a racehorse for £5,000 minutes before it ran in Montreal – then watched as it came in fourth and dropped dead.

TURNING OVER A NEW LEAF

The Waterloo Hurdle at Haydock Park on 9 December 1992 had to be re-started after the entire field took the wrong course. As they set off, the jockeys found the second hurdle blocked off by marker dolls and so they by-passed it. They continued on their way but confusion spread through their ranks as they debated whether they had done the right thing. Jockey Richard Dunwoody said later: 'I was pretty sure we should have jumped it, but the others carried on and I daren't stop in case I was wrong.' Trainer David Nicholson dashed on to the course to tell them to stop as they passed the stands but most kept going until they had completed a full circuit. At that point, they pulled up. Eventually the race was re-started to include the hurdle in question. The stewards held an inquiry into the fiasco and discovered that it had been caused by a groundsman accidentally turning over two pages in his racecard. Thinking the race was a chase, he had blocked off the wrong obstacle.

MISGUIDED ENTHUSIASM

Lord Derby's Fairway, reckoned to be the best three-year-old in the country, was 3/1 favourite for the 1928 Derby. But the horse's chance vanished long before the race had started when he was mobbed by well-wishers as he left the paddock, to the extent that hairs were plucked from his tail. Given the enthusiasm of the souvenir hunters, he was lucky not to end up as a gelding. Needless to say, the horse was petrified by the experience and began sweating profusely. And he came nowhere in the race.

O'SULLEVAN LOSES BUT WINS

Racing commentator Peter O'Sullevan has enjoyed the privilege of owning some superb racehorses in his time but in his book *Calling The Horses*, he recalled the other side of the coin. Back in the early 1950s, he owned a horse called Fidonia which, although once useful, had become distinctly one-paced in its later years. Following a mile-and-a-half race at Lewes in June 1953 in which Fidonia was well and truly tailed off, jockey John Hislop had caustically remarked that the horse 'went well for the first hundred yards.' On 1 August, it took part in an amateur riders' race at Warwick and O'Sullevan bet the trainer of a rival horse £1 that Fidonia would be last. He knew he was on to a winner with his loser. Fidonia was again tailed off, leaving jockey Vic Wark, who had conscientiously walked the course beforehand, to remark that he had probably covered the ground faster on foot in the morning than he had on horseback in the afternoon!

A CASE OF INTERFERENCE

*T*hese days, horses have only to come close together for an objection to be lodged for interference. But even the most serious instance of bumping pales in comparison to the treatment apparently dished out to Irish horse Rust in the 1839 Grand National. That year's race became famous as the one in which Captain Becher ended up in the brook but there was plenty of other drama at Aintree that day, some of which was tantamount to skullduggery. In the wake of the Captain's demise, the race looked all set to be won by Willie McDonough on Rust until the other jockeys manoeuvred him down a lane where a crowd of spectators with vested interests deliberately hemmed him in until the field was well clear. This is the equivalent of Sebastian Coe being kidnapped half-way through the 800 metres and not released until the other runners were in the home straight. More than a little peeved at what had happened , Rust's connections protested long and loud. But their objections fell on deaf ears and Lottery was declared the winner. The record books list Rust as 'pulled up'.

BROWNED OFF

At the start of the 1985 Champion Hurdle at Cheltenham, 4/6 favourite Browne's Gazette swerved violently left as the tape rose, forfeiting twenty lengths and all chance of the race. Jockey Dermot Browne (no relation) was much criticized afterwards. He explained: 'As we were lining up, he almost took off and looked like charging the tape so I turned him round and shouted to the starter but I was on the far side of him and other jockeys were also shouting. He couldn't have heard me because as I was turning round to my left, he let them go.' Trainer Monica Dickinson had a different view of the events. 'Dermot was caught napping. He should have charged the tape so there would have been a false start and they could have begun again. He'll remember this race for a long time.'

LOST IN THE TRANSLATION

Affectionately known as 'Big Pete', trainer Peter Walwyn was celebrating a victory with French owner Marc Laloum. Basking in his success, M. Laloum announced that he wished to dispense with the formality of surnames and said, 'Je m'appelle Marc', to which Walwyn replied, 'Je m'appelle Grand Pete.' French scholars will confirm that the literal translation of Grand Pete is, unfortunately, Big Fart!

DOUBLE BLOW

On 22 April 1993, an odds-on punter bet £15,000 on Jizyah (1–10) and £18,000 on Carbon Steel (2–17), both at Catterick. It wasn't his day. In the 2.45, Jizyah finished second of two and just over an hour later, Carbon Steel trailed in last of three.

DEVON LOCH

Of all Grand National losers, the unluckiest was undoubtedly the Queen Mother's Devon Loch in 1956. Clear on the run-in and being urged home by a roar of approval in anticipation of a Royal victory, Devon Loch was less than 50 yards from the winning post when he inexplicably spreadeagled on the flat. It appeared that he had lifted his forelegs as if to jump a non-existent obstacle before realizing his error. While the crowd watched aghast, the well-beaten E.S.B passed the stricken Devon Loch to claim the prize. Devon Loch's jockey, Dick Francis, said of the aftermath: 'It was quiet in the Royal box. Their Majesties tried to comfort me and said what a beautiful race Devon Loch had run; and in my turn I tried to say how desperately sorry I was that we had not managed to cover those last vital 50 yards.' If nothing else, the mystery surrounding Devon Loch's failure fired Dick Francis's imagination and helped him to become a highly successful thriller writer.

FREEMAN'S FOLLY

In days of old, the welcome for southern jockeys at northern racecourses was usually heated rather than warm. And so it was when Dave Dick and Arthur Freeman journeyed to the County Durham outpost of Sedgefield. Changing before the race, Freeman had made the mistake of allowing his over-confidence to get the better of him. He went so far as to tell Dick that they had the race between them since the local jockeys were all useless. As Freeman spoke, Dick spotted a wizened little man listening intently. Come the race, Freeman's mount looked a certain winner until, between the last two fences, the old man Dick had seen ranged up alongside and, leaning over, coolly removed the bridle from Freeman's horse. 'Now let's see you ride a finish,

sonny,' cackled the senior citizen as he urged his steed to victory. *It's fair to say that from then on Freeman was a little more cautious in voicing his opinions on northern jockeys.*

COUP BACKFIRE

The notorious swindler Horatio Bottomley thought he was on to a certainty when he tried to fix a three-runner selling race. But his plans were shot to pieces when the horse which he had arranged to win suddenly dropped dead in running. This left the other two jockeys whom he had bribed at a complete loss as to what they were supposed to do...

POTTY PUNTER

Betting-mad Brian Bonnay was so keen to put £50 on a hot tip that he ran nine miles to the bookies along a high-speed railway line. He had an account with a bookmaker in

Northallerton but, after missing his train from Darlington, was worried that he wouldn't be able to get it on in time. So Brian, a half-marathon runner, jumped on to the East Coast main line and began to jog the 14 miles to Northallerton in order to place a bet on Express Service in the 2.50 at Lingfield. It was an appropriate choice of name since for the next nine miles, Brian recklessly dodged across the tracks, forcing InterCity expresses to slow down to 20 mph. At one point, he even stopped to ask startled track workers whether he was going the right way for Northallerton. Eventually, he was apprehended by the Transport Police and fined £40 with £100 costs for trespassing on the railway. Later he admitted: 'I was wrong but I had a great tip.' It wasn't worth the effort. The horse came nowhere.

LORD'S LAMENT

In a race at Cheltenham in 1964, John Oaksey cleared the second last on Pioneer Spirit almost a fence ahead. Success seemed a formality until the noble Lord got it into his head that he had somehow taken the wrong course and decided to pull Pioneer Spirit up. In fact, he had not taken the wrong course at all and the only other survivor, Bill Tellwright, swept past on his way to an unexpected victory with what Oaksey described as 'a look of mingled pity and contempt'. On arriving at the finish, Oaksey was roundly booed by the crowd and the stewards completed his misery by fining him £25.

PAYNE'S PAIN

The worst judge of horse flesh was surely a 19th century dealer by the name of Payne. He desperately tried to get rid of a horse called Magnum Bonum which, in fairness, had proved abysmal on the flat. Time and time again, the animal was returned to him and once he was even offered £50 to take it back! It seemed as if he would be stuck with the useless chestnut for life until, against all the odds, Quartermaine, a fellow dealer from Piccadilly, showed a glimmer of interest. Each time money was discussed, Quartermaine offered less but by then Payne was just so relieved to see the back of the horse that he accepted. Quartermaine took one look at Magnum Bonum, renamed it Discount and it promptly won the 1844 Grand National.

PASTA CARING

One of the most novel ideas in recent years is the World Jockeys' Championship, the first of which took place at Cheltenham in April 1984. But whilst our trainers are adept at dishing out riding instructions in their native tongue, for some there was a definite breakdown in communications when it came to addressing jockeys from overseas. A case in point was John Edwards for whom the then Italian champion Giannantonio Colleo was riding Misty Dale. Edwards sought to get round the problem by borrowing an interpreter from the local Spaghetti House but it seems extremely doubtful whether Colleo understood a word of the race plan. For when he returned beaten, he was facing a roasting from Edwards and waiter for disobeying riding orders. They could have saved their breath because he didn't understand the verbal lashing either.

NO EARLY PACE

The 1949 Midland St. Leger Trial at Birmingham must hold the record for the slowest horse race ever run...or rather walked. There were only two entrants – Gordon Richards on

Ridge Wood and Tommy Lowrey on Courier. Both jockeys were under strict instructions not to make the pace under any circumstances so when the tape rose, both froze to the spot. With the crowd beside themselves with apathy, Courier actually turned round to face the opposite direction. Realising that the next race would soon be due off, the starter began to lose patience and sent his assistant to crack the whip. This action galvanized jockeys and steeds into some sort of forward movement and they broke into a slow canter, covering the first furlong in nearly a minute and a half. To a chorus of jeers, they passed the stands with Ridge Wood winning the one mile five furlong event in 5min 14sec, more than twice the time it usually takes to cover such a distance. As evidence that the afternoon stroll took very little out of the winner, Ridge Wood went on to win the St. Leger itself that year.

OFF TOO SOON

This year was by no means the first Grand National to have suffered starting difficulties. In 1951 starter Leslie Firth pressed the lever releasing the barrier while over half of the runners were still milling around in search of a suitable position. No false start recall signal was given and so there was a mad rush to make up lost ground. Because of this cavalry charge, 12 horses, a third of the field, came to grief within the first half mile. The race never properly recovered and only two finished.

DAM USELESS

Rheingold's dam Athene was by no means the swiftest horse in the world. Indeed such was her failure rate on the racecourse that as a two-year-old she was given away as first prize in a raffle!

DANGEROUS DENTURES

Jockey Josh Gifford looked to have a race at his mercy until an awkward jump at the last resulted in his false teeth plate getting stuck in his throat. With Gifford unable to concentrate wholly on riding out the finish, the race was lost.

POINT OF NO RETURN

Due to run in the first race at Folkestone, Tony Hide's filly Magnetic Point was loaded into a horsebox bound for Southwell by mistake. The error was not discovered until half a mile from the Nottinghamshire Course by which time it was too late to get her to Folkestone.

NO HOPE OF RECOVERY

Having developed a keen interest in racing, an Indian ruler set about starting up a stud in 1874. He was particularly keen on a horse called Recovery and offered a sizeable sum for the horse to stand as a stallion. Sad to say, Recovery was a bit of a non-starter at stud since he had undergone a little operation from which he was unlikely to recover – he was a gelding.

G-G-G-GLORIOUS GOODWOOD

The authorities at Goodwood in 1830 made an unfortunate choice of starter. They selected a man with a fearful stutter which was so pronounced when he became excited that he was hardly able to speak at all. That year, there were a number of false starts to the Duke of Richmond's Plate, causing a length delay. After the race was finally run, William Arnull, the senior jockey in the field, was summoned by the stewards to explain the reason for the inactivity at the start. His reply was: 'Some of the horses were no doubt restive, but in my opinion the fault lay chiefly with the starter. He is just like an old firelock which fizzles ever so long in the pan before it goes off, and when he did get the word out, there was no knowing whether he said "Go!" or "No!"'

PERMANENTLY UNPLACED

Mick Easterby reckons the worst horse he ever trained was one named Mick 'n' Dick which he co-owned with a neighbouring farmer. Apparently Dick was so excited about the prospect of seeing the animal in action that he didn't sleep for four nights before its racecourse debut. If only the horse had been as geed-up for as Easterby said: 'We didn't make the first ten then and we didn't make the first ten ever. The consolation was that after his fourth run, Dick was sleeping sound as a bell.'

EDDIE'S ERROR

At the second last in the 1948 Grand National, First of the Dandies was joined in the lead by 100–1 shot Zahia, seemingly full of running. But after landing safely, Zahia's jockey, Eddie Reavey, mistook the course and to the amazement of spectators and fellow jockeys alike, he directed Zahia wide of the final fence. Not that First of the Dandies was the one to profit since it was overhauled on the run-in by Sheila's Cottage.

UNSOUND ADVICE

Before the 1965 Champion Hurdle, George Todd, trainer of the quietly-fancied Nosey, instructed his jockey to track

Salmon Spray as he was 'the best jumper in the race'. Salmon Spray repaid the compliment by standing-off too far at the second flight. The outcome was that he landed on top of the hurdle and crumpled to the ground, bringing down Nosey!

DIDN'T READ THE SMALL PRINT

Edward Hodson of Wolverhampton thought his dreams had come true when he landed a 3,956,748 to 1 bet for a 55p stake on 11 February 1984. He couldn't wait to get down to his local bookmaker to collect his winnings. Working it all out on a calculator, he reckoned it would come to around a cool £2 million. So he marched into the shop, thrust his betting slip over the counter and was quietly reminded that the bookmaker had a payout limit of £3,000.

STUDENT OF FORM

One racegoer spent so long studying the form that he ruined the actual race. It was a three-horse contest for four-year-olds and upwards at the Curragh but with the horses up at the start, our man was studying the conditions of the race when he noticed that the hot favourite St. Dunstan was a three-year-old and was therefore not qualified to run. Bell H was hastily installed as favourite although the jockeys, at their distant location, knew nothing of these remarkable developments. The race started and Bell H disputed the lead with St. Dunstan with the third runner, Marble Hall, lagging behind by some way. Then suddenly, Bell H swerved across the course, crashed into a stone bollard and broke his neck. St. Dunstan had already been disqualified before the start so the only horse left to award the race to was the outsider Marble Hall. But the pernickety punter was not done yet. Once more he stepped forward, this time to point out that Marble Hall's jockey was not qualified to ride. So with no winner, the race was declared void.

A MARS A DAY...

Gelding No Bombs romped home by eight lengths in a 1979 race at Ascot, only to be disqualified after a routine dope test revealed traces of caffeine and theobromine. It transpired that a Mars Bar was to blame, the horse having snatched one from his stable boy on the way to the races. Trainer Peter Easterby said ruefully: 'That's the most expensive Mars Bar ever – it cost £4,064 in prize money.'

LAST-FENCE DISASTER

Riding the front-running 100–1 outsider Davy Jones in the 1936 Grand National, the Honourable Anthony (later Lord) Mildmay was enjoying a spectacular round and nearing the finish, had the rest of the field stretched. But for some reason he had failed to take the precaution of knotting the end of his reins. At the second last, well clear of the opposition, Davy Jones made his only mistake and pecked slightly on landing. Mildmay correctly allowed the reins to slip through his hands but the buckle had come undone and suddenly he was powerless to steer the horse. As a result, Davy Jones veered left at the final fence and ran out, scattering spectators in his wake. Reynoldstown gratefully accepted the opportunity to win for the second successive year. But the hapless Mildmay was not forgotten and the ordinary chase course at Aintree was subsequently known as the Mildmay Course.

BROUGHT DOWN BY HORSELESS JOCKEY

Wheal Prosper and Mick Fitzgerald looked all over the winners of a race at Newton Abbot on 14 December 1992 until they came unstuck at the last. This surely handed the race to Hywel Davies on board Troubador Boy who appeared only to have to jump the final fence. Troubador Boy cleared it well enough but as the horse landed, a dazed Fitzgerald staggered to his feet and sent Troubador Boy crashing to the ground. Luckless trainer Tim Thomson-Jones said: 'Mick hobbled into the weighing room looking for a bit of sympathy but all he got was an earful from Hywel.'

HOPELESS HORSE

Noted Victorian actor/manager Lewis Waller was persuaded to enter the world of horse racing by an Irish trainer. At the time, Waller's play Monsieur Beaucaire was playing to packed houses so he commissioned the trainer to buy a horse which he then named Beaucaire. On the racecourse, Beaucaire dismally failed to bask in his owner's reflected glory and was soon despatched to an early retirement. Some time later, the trainer met Waller and asked whether he knew what had happened to the horse. 'I saw him only the other day in a hansom,' replied Waller. 'He drove me to Waterloo – and I missed my train!'

FULL OF RUNNING

The Duke of Portland's horse Roche Abbey was still so full of running after winning the 1909 Singleton Plate at Goodwood that it couldn't be stopped. It galloped on up St. Roche's Hill, unseated its jockey and disappeared over the brow of The Trundle. The disconsolate rider dusted himself down and returned to base but was unable to weigh-in since the saddle which he was supposed to be carrying had last been seen heading for the Hampshire border.

ATHLETICS

THE ULTIMATE SHAME

Wallace Williams of the Virgin Islands was under no illusions about his athletic prowess. He certainly didn't expect to win the marathon in the 1979 Pan American Games at San Juan but as a gallant loser, having trudged 26 miles in scorching heat, he felt sure of a warm reception from the crowd in the stadium. As he wearily approached the stadium in last place, by now nearly 39 minutes behind the previous finisher, he thought the crowd were strangely silent. Perhaps, he reasoned, they were saving themselves to greet his heroic entrance. Then he realized why all was quiet. The stadium door was locked. Everyone had gone home.

RAN IN BOOTS

In the 1936 Olympic marathon in Berlin, Manuel Dias of Portugal was lying second after 17 kilometres but then began to pay for his decision to wear new running shoes for the race. The state of his feet deteriorated rapidly, to the point where he felt compelled to throw away the offending shoes at 20 kilometres. Not relishing the prospect of completing the course in bare feet, Dias sought out a spectator willing to lend him some footwear. Unfortunately, the only person Dias could find was a boy from the Hitler youth movement who lent him his heavy boots! Naturally this didn't exactly boost his medal hopes but he goose-stepped his way home to finish 17th.

LOST MEDAL

Russian athlete Ivanon Vyacheslav was so thrilled to win a gold medal at the 1956 Melbourne Olympics that he hurled the medal high into the air in jubilation. Unfortunately it came down in Lake Wendouree where, despite a frantic search by Vyacheslav and his team-mates, it probably remains to this day.

THE LONG RUN

*O*ne of the epic journeys in Olympic history was undertaken by Italian Carlo Airoldi in order to compete in the 1896 Games in Athens. Setting off on foot from his home in Milan on 28 February, he reached Ragusa in Yugoslavia on 19 March, having covered the 695 miles at an astonishing average of 33 miles per day. On the night of 23 March he boarded a boat via Corfu to Patrasso where he arrived four days later. Then it was back to pounding the rough roads until five days and 136 miles on, he finally made it to Athens. Proud of his achievement and high on expectation, Airoldi handed in his Olympic entry...only for it to be refused because it had been alleged that he was a professional.

CAYMAN FLYERS

At the 1982 Commonwealth Games in Brisbane, the entire Cayman Islands team consisted of just two athletes, both of whom competed in the men's 10,000 metres. This pair were not the most fleet-footed of individuals and often succeeded in hindering the other runners on the many occasions on which they were lapped. As they trudged round, they did at least receive encouragement from above with a light aircraft towing a banner urging them to yet greater efforts. The response was immediate and David Bonn surged home in 41min 21.50 s, a mere matter of over 13 minutes behind the winner.

WRONG TURN

With just five kilometres to go, nineteen-year-old Swede Ernst Fast was comfortably ahead in the 1900 Olympic marathon in Paris when he and his accompanying cyclist took a wrong turning. By the time Fast had recovered, his hopes were gone and he had to settle for third place.

CEREMONIAL CHAOS

The opening ceremony of the 1908 Olympics in London was a testimony to British organization. All the national flags were meant to be fluttering around the White City Stadium but, possibly due to geographical defects among the committee, the powers that be forgot to include such minor countries as Sweden and the United States. The Americans in particular took umbrage and responded by refusing to dip the Stars and Stripes to King Edward at the march past. To add to the fun, the Finns flatly refused to march behind the flag of Czarist Russia and so came into the stadium without any banner at all.

PENSIONER POWER

The least competitive athletics event in history was probably the over-89 age group in the 1989 World Veterans' Championship staged at Eugene, Oregon. The star of the show was 94-year-old Wang Ching Chang from Taiwan who took gold medals in the 100 metres, 200 metres, shot putt and javelin. But in each of these events, Chang faced no more than one opponent – the comparatively youthful but perennial runner-up, 90-year-old Herbert Kirk from Montana. Observers agreed that Chang's greater experience won the day.

TEA BREAK

Following the run of a lifetime in the 1938 Natal provincial marathon, South African Johannes Coleman stormed across the finishing line at Alexander Park, Pietermaritzburg, confident that he had shattered the world record. At the time it stood at 2hr 26min 42s and on entering the park, Coleman's own watch had shown 2hr 23min. So as he burst the tape, he eagerly sought out the chief time-keeper for ratification. Alas, he could only be found in the nearby tea-room, calmly taking refreshment. When a peeved Coleman asked him what on earth he was doing there, the official apologized saying that nobody had expected any of the runners to arrive back so soon!

CARELESS KERRY

As the world record holder, Australia's Kerry O'Brien was a hot tip to win the 3,000 metres steeplechase at the 1970 Commonwealth Games in Edinburgh. All was going according to the script until on the last lap, he made the elementary mistake of falling at the water jump, allowing his unfancied team-mate Tony Hanning to take the gold.

LATE ARRIVAL

Travelling to the 1896 Olympics, the United States team turned up days late, having forgotten that the Greeks still used the Julian calendar and were thus 11 days in advance

MIST-ERY TOUR

Dozens of runners in a 13-mile half-marathon at Newton Aycliffe, County Durham, ended up doing as many as 20 miles after getting hopelessly lost in the fog. Many knocked on doors of houses pleading for directions while one runner, who had wandered seven miles off course, called into a pub and asked puzzled regulars: 'Can you tell me the way to the finishing line?' They obligingly drew him a map. Race organizer Chris White said a new venue for the annual event had confused a number of the competitors. 'They didn't realize that the first and last mile were on the same stretch of road, and headed back out into the countryside. I think the weather then began to affect their judgement. And councillors were also partly to blame for not letting us put up proper directions.' Sunderland Harrier Dave Wyatt was in the lead before he too went astray. He eventually crossed the finishing line 30 minutes after the first runner home. But in keeping with the splendid confusion of this event, Chris White explained: 'The poor lad did so well running an extra five miles that we gave him the race.'

SPECTATOR INVOLVEMENT

Competing in the 1900 Olympics, reigning discus champion Robert Garrett of the United States put all three of his throws into the crowd. He thus found it difficult to retain his title.

AND HERE COMES WOSSISNAME

*W*hen Gidamis Shahanga of Tanzania was the first person to enter the stadium at the end of the 1978 Commonwealth Games marathon in Edmonton, everyone was reduced to total silence. For nobody seemed to have a clue who he was. Television and radio reporters thumbed through their programme notes and scratched their heads in puzzlement while even many of the Tanzanian team management weren't sure of his identity! But a lap later, they were hailing the unknown runner as a new national hero.

THE ITALIAN JOB

*F*or the 1908 Olympics in London, the distance of the marathon was extended by an extra 385 yards so that the race would finish in front of the Royal box at the White City.

But this additional yardage proved the undoing of little Italian Dorando Pietri. On a day of sweltering heat, he was first in the stadium but began to falter when he lost momentum on the downward ramp leading on to the cinder track. His cause was not helped when he was directed left instead of right as he had been expecting. This led him to stumble, an act which he repeated four more times while his sagging legs attempted to carry him around the final part-lap of the track. His last collapse was a matter of yards from the line right in front of the Royal box. Whether or not the over-zealous officials deemed this to be an inappropriate sight for the King or whether they acted out of pure concern for the runner's safety is open to speculation, but they instantly rushed to Pietri's assistance and helped him over the finish line. Then they disqualified him. The gold medal eventually went to the runner-up, American Johnny Hayes, who crossed the line 32 seconds later. As consolation for missing out on the medal, Pietri was presented with an inscribed gold cup.

SORRY, LADS

Americans Eddie Hart and Rey Robinson were two of the hot favourites for the 100 metres at the 1972 Munich Olympics. So it was probably to the disguised delight of their rivals that the pair failed to appear for the second-round heats. What had caused the absence? A mystery bug? Political intervention? No, their coach had mis-red the starting time.

THE PITS!

Preparations were so poor for the 1900 Olympics in Paris that the competitors in the long jump, triple jump and other field events had to dig their own pits.

TRAINING HITCH

Keen to fit in a spot of last-minute training on the day before the 1930 Commonwealth Games marathon in Hamilton, Canada, English record holder Harry Payne was hit by a car and had to miss the race.

MINI MARATHON

The least successful attempt to cheat at the Olympics was carried out by American Fred Lorz in the 1904 Games at St. Louis. As the spectators in the stadium awaited the return of the marathon runners, the sprightly figure of Lorz bounded in looking remarkably fresh. The patriotic crowd erupted, little knowing that they were the victims of a hoax. It was only when the real winner, fellow countryman Thomas Hicks, arrived looking tired and dishevelled, that officials began to query Lorz's physical state. Then it emerged that after dropping out with cramp early on in the race, Lorz had accepted a lift in a car for over half the distance. When the car also broke down about four miles from the stadium, Lorz resumed running to milk his applause. At first, Lorz was banned for life for his misdemeanour but he insisted that it was only a joke and that he would have owned up in time.

HOT STUFF

The 1933 South African 10 Mile Championship was held in such blistering heat that none of the runners finished!

PIPPED

Few athletes can have had a more cavalier attitude to winning an Olympic medal than Felix Carvajal, a Cuban postal carrier competing in the 1904 marathon. In the end he finished fourth but would undoubtedly have been among the medals had he not stopped to talk to spectators or eat some unripe fruit which slowed his progress somewhat. What's more, it was 72 years before Cuba had enother entrant in the Olympic marathon.

LEAST SUCCESSFUL CELEBRATION

Thrilled by his gold medal triumph in the 400 metres hurdles at the 1974 Commonwealth Games in Christchurch, Alan Pascoe thought he would do a little lap of honour as a treat for the British spectators in the stadium and for all those watching at home. Nothing too ambitious – just a standing leap over a hurdle. But he had grossly under-estimated how tired his legs were and, to the amusement of millions of viewers, three times he tried to clear the obstacle and three times he failed, finally ending up in an undignified heap on the track. Increasingly battered and bruised, he was wisely advised to give up before putting himself out for the rest of the year. Later he explained: 'My head and heart were willing but I'm afraid my legs weren't.'

DIRECTIONAL DIFFICULTIES

At the end of the gruelling marathon in the 1954 European Championships in Berne, Russian athlete Ivan Filin strode into the stadium clear of Finland's Veikko Karvonen. But once inside the stadium, the Soviet runner turned the wrong way. He lost over 100 metres before he realized his error and by the time he had got back on course, the best he could manage was third place.

LAP FLAP

John Savidan of New Zealand thought he had timed his finishing burst to perfection at the end of the six mile race at the 1930 British Empire Games in Hamilton, Canada. Unfortunately, a mistake by the lap counting official meant there was still one more circuit to go!

WENT ON PICNIC

The 1912 Olympic marathon in Stockholm was staged on a particularly warm day, to the despair of Japan's Shinzo Kanaguri. Consequently, when he spotted a family relaxing in their roadside garden, he decided that looked preferable to running another ten or so miles. So he dropped out of the race and joined them. Suitably refreshed, he then made his way back to his homeland – without informing any Olympic officials. For some years afterwards, it was rumoured that they were still searching for him in the Swedish forests.

THE LAST POST

It seems that marathons have an uncanny knack of being run on the hottest days of the year. The 1954 Commonwealth Games event in Vancouver was yet another example. This was the race in which Jim Peters collapsed in the stadium but there was also high drama surrounding the second English runner, Stan Cox. He too suffered from sun-stroke and met an untimely end when he ran into a telegraph pole.

SLOW START

Nerves were really on edge at the beginning of the Olympic 100 metres final in 1912. There were an incredible eight false starts before Ralph Craig of the United States was able to race to victory.

EVERY LITTLE HELPS

When it comes to staging any international games, fund-raising is all important. So when New Zealand announced that the 1990 Commonwealth Games would cost in the region of £10 million, they were possibly hoping to attract a few sizeable contributions. The organizers were particularly excited at the swift response from a group of ladies in Christchurch offering financial assistance. That initial enthusiasm waned a little when they heard that the ladies' master-plan for raising the millions was to run a cake stall.

HOLLOW VICTORY

The four-man line-up for the final of the 400 metres in the London Olympics of 1908 consisted of three Americans and one Briton, Lieutenant Wyndham Halswelle. One of the Americans, Carpenter, won the race but the British judges accused them of ganging up on our chap, thereby impeding him. So they took it upon themselves to disqualify Carpenter and ordered a re-run for the following day. The Americans decided that if this was the British interpretation of the Olympic spirit, they could keep it and refused to have anything more to do with the final. And so Halswelle triumphantly took the gold by virtue of a walk-over.

TWO STRIDES FROM VICTORY

At the 1970 Commonwealth Games in Edinburgh, New Zealand's Sylvia Potts was just two strides from winning the ladies' 1500 metres gold when she fell. By the time she had regained her feet, she was ninth.

THE SOUND OF SILENCE

Finishing sixth and last in the 1951 Asian Games marathon in New Delhi, Japan's Oichi Noda arrived at the stadium to find that everyone had gone home with the exception of the two officials left to clock him in. It was scarcely surprising that the crowd had long since departed, the winner having crossed the line a whole hour earlier.

NAME THAT TUNE

*O*fficials at the 1952 Helsinki Olympics were taken by
surprise when Luxembourg's Josef Bartel won the gold
medal in the 1500 metres. With Luxembourg being perennial
losers at just about everything, naturally enough nobody
expected them to gain a medal. And so when it came to the
victory ceremony, there was no trace anywhere of the score
of the Luxembourg national anthem. An embarrassing delay
ensued before the musicians struck up a hurried improvised
version. But nobody knew whether or not it sounded like
the original.

MOTOR SPORT

MOST BORING GRAND PRIX

As an exercise in tedium, nothing could match the 1926 French Motor Racing Grand Prix at Miramas. Spectators arrived to find that the field consisted of just three cars. Nor was there much scope for rival support since all three were Bugattis. Still, they thought, perhaps the lack of numbers would be compensated for by a really exciting race. Wrong. Only one car completed the seemingly endless 100 laps, the second finished 15 laps behind and the third retired.

DIDN'T GET FAR

The start of the London to Mexico Rally in 1970 was going to be a great sporting spectacle. The cars would set off from Wembley and arrive in Mexico City in time for the finals of the World Cup. As an added attraction, the organizers recruited England manager Sir Alf Ramsey to start the event. He flagged away the first car to embark on this tortuous 16,000 mile endurance test of man and machine, anticipating the roar of the engine and the clouds of smoke from the exhaust as it disappeared into the distance. Instead it jerkily chugged along and finally broke down after just 100 yards.

LEAST SUCCESSFUL RACING CAR

*O*ver the years, all the talk of Mercedes, Ferrari, McLaren and Williams has rather obscured the achievements in Formula One motor racing of the Scarab. Perhaps it has been denied its place in the Hall of Fame because it sounds more like something you pick than drive. Or then again its omission could be attributed to the fact that it was so embarrassingly slow, not after all the ideal requisite for a Grand Prix car. The Scarab factory was started by Lance Reventlow in California in 1957 and the sports cars equipped themselves so favourably against European invaders that it was decided to develop a car to enter the realms of Formula One. After two long years of research and testing, the motor racing world held its breath as the Formula One Scarab was unveiled in the 1960 Monaco Grand Prix. Sadly, its appearance was restricted to the qualifying laps on that occasion since it was nowhere near fast enough to make it on to the grid for the race itself. Undeterred, drivers Reventlow and Chuck Haigh finally managed to qualify for the Belgian Grand Prix that year...but both had to withdraw before the start with engine trouble. And after those two attempts, a career in which it failed to compete in a Grand Prix in anger, the Scarab vanished from Formula One, never to be seen again.*

SHEEP SHUNTER

A motor racing enthusiast by the name of Maurice Geoghegan, who lived in the Northamptonshire village of Silverstone, thought it would be a wonderful idea to stage a race on a nearby disused airfield. The event took place in September 1947 but sadly Maurice's participation ended early on when his Frazer Nash car was in collision with a hefty, slow-moving sheep which chose an unwise moment to cross the circuit. Thereafter, the race became known as the Mutton Grand Prix.

FAWLTY MACHINE

In the 1922 Isle Of Man TT, Freddie Dixon was lying in second place when he suffered a puncture on the last lap. Graham Walker, who was to finish fifth, recalled seeing Dixon near Ramsey 'jumping up and down on his rear wheel, with his arms stretched to the heavens and his mouth working with unheard oaths.'

ASCARI SAW THE LIGHT

The Ferrari driven by the legendary Alberto Ascari crashed out within just 15 minutes of the start of the epic Mille Miglia road race in 1951. It was four o'clock in the morning when Ascari was distracted by a spectator who shone a light on his car to read the race number. As a result, Ascari failed to spot a patch of oil on the road. He was so furious that he refused to enter the event the following year.

SECOND BEST

Only six drivers in history have competed in more Grands Prix than the Italian Andrea de Cesaris. Since 1980, he has driven in over 170 but has yet to win, his best position being runner-up.

STUNT BACKFIRED

The Trans-African Rally had to be shelved during the 1960s because of the continent's various political upheavals but in 1967 Ford mounted a single-car publicity 'race' from Cape Town to Britain between a Corsair and the Windsor Castle liner. Whilst the ship enjoyed a relatively trouble-free passage, the Corsair had to be air-lifted for over 1,000 miles to avoid certain 'no-go' areas. But the support crew landed in the Congo before the car and were immediately arrested as South African spies. They were forced to spend several days in jail before they were able to talk their way out of their predicament.

KEVIN'S CLANGER

Australian Kevin Magee thought he had done the hard part when finishing fourth in the 500cc US Motor Cycle Grand Prix at Laguna Seca, California, on 16 April 1989. But while waving to the crowds on his lap of honour, he came off his machine and broke a leg.

NO FINISHERS

The trophy presentation for the 1972 Bandama Rally in West Africa must have been the shortest on record since there were no finishers. This was partly because the rally organizers had set a ridiculously tight driving schedule which they were determined to adhere to at all costs. The last two drivers left in the event, Tony Fall and Shekhar Mehta, simply ran out of time and with the organizers still not prepared to amend the schedule by granting a few extra minutes, officially nobody finished.

SLIPPED UP

The Wembley track was not exactly at its best for the finals of the 1975 World Speedway Championship. A lack of use and a lack of rain had turned it into little more than a dust bowl. This proved too much for some fans who, choked by clouds of shale, jumped the barriers and turned on the hoses. Ironically, this decisive action was to prove the downfall of home-grown favourite Peter Collins. By Heat Nine, Collins represented England's brightest hope of a world title for years but his chances were wrecked when he floundered in a sodden patch of track, one which had been drenched by the irate crowd.

WRONG INFORMATION

During the last hour of the 1935 Le Mans 24-Hour Race, the Alfa Romeo driven by Rene-Louis Dreyfus made up a vast amount of ground on the leading car, the Lagonda of John Hindmarsh and Louis Fontes. The Lagonda was a very sick machine and had been forced to make several stops suffering from fading oil pressure. Dreyfus seemed assured of victory and when he was told by his pits that he had passed the Lagonda, he decided to slow right down and coast home at his leisure, knowing that nothing could catch him. So when the chequered flag was shown, Dreyfus was fully expecting to be proclaimed the winner, only to discover that the pits had made a mistake and he was still nearly a lap behind the ailing Lagonda!

POINTLESS

American Brett Lunger drove in a total of 34 Grands Prix between 1975 and 1978 without gaining a single point.

ODD DISCOVERY

D riving an old Bugatti in the 1945 Bois de Boulogne race, Frenchman Maurice Trintignant was dismayed when the car 'died' of fuel starvation. But that was nothing to his reaction when he learned that the cause was an over-accumulation of rat droppings at the bottom of the fuel tank. Obviously, while the car had sat idly during the war, the fuel tank had become home to generations of rodents. From then on, Trintignant was affectionately nicknamed 'petoulet' meaning 'rat dropping'. It may not be the sort of name you would wish to be greeted with at a party but at least it is an iota more original than 'Gazza'.

16-CAR PILE-UP

T he Indianapolis 500 has never exactly been a race for the faint-hearted, the only comparable spectacle in this country being London's Park Lane in rush hour. The 1966 '500' was particularly memorable in that it had to be stopped after just three seconds following a 16-car pile-up. A wall of 33 cars had hurtled into the first corner where they proceeded to bounce off one another like a bad day at the dodgems. When the dust had settled, it took 30 minutes to clear the wreckage.

DOGGED BY BAD LUCK

In the early days of motor racing, it was nothing for a Grand Prix to be held over two days. A typically long-winded event was the 1921 French Grand Prix at Dieppe. American driver David Bruce-Brown held a handy 11-second advantage on the second day...until he hit a stray dog and damaged his fuel tank. Dog and driver were in a similar position – both had lost their lead. Bruce-Brown was forced to resort to illicit wayside refuelling which later resulted in his disqualification.

WATERY GRAVE

The 1907 Peking to Paris race was won by Prince Scipione Borghese, an Italian nobleman, driving an Itala. It had been an eventful journey. At one point the car had plunged off a rickety bridge into a ravine and had to be winched out by a gang of Siberian railway workers. Even so, despite stopping over for three days in Moscow presumably to take in the sights, the Prince finished an easy winner. The successful Itala car was in great demand. It was shown at the 1908 Olympia Motor Show but met an untimely end when, en route to being shipped to New York for another exhibition, it rolled into the dockside water at Genoa. The car was eventually salvaged but was badly damaged. Thus the Itala goes down in history as being the only car to survive a 10,000 mile rally but not the subsequent exhibition.

PLAN WRECKED

Prior to the Diamond Jubilee 50cc race at the 1967 TT, Suzuki riders Graham and Anscheidt had been instructed that team-mate Yoshiwa Katayuma was to win to enable Suzuki to claim an all-Japanese victory. But that was easier said than done. Firstly, Katayuma made a poor start which meant that the other two had to hang around waiting for him to catch up. When Katayuma did finally make up the lost ground, he spotted an oil leak on Anscheidt's machine. As he rode alongside to take a closer look, he fell off. With Katayuma failing miserably to re-start his bike, Graham decided to abandon the pre-race plan and went on to win.

CLOSE TO HOME

A popular type of event in the 1920s was the Concours d'Elegance, a form of rally in which drivers had to motor from far afield, usually at a maximum average speed of 20 mph. The winner was whoever drove the furthest. For one such Concours in 1928, the 'rallying point' was the Lancashire town of Clitheroe after which a strict average speed of 20 mph had to be maintained to the finish at Southport. Competitors could choose to start from a selection of venues. There were 20 in Britain as well as Brussels and Paris. The majority of entrants, relishing a true challenge, set off from either John O'Groats or Land's End but one driver, somewhat lacking in pioneering spirit, actually chose Clitheroe as his starting point! And even then he probably wouldn't have turned out if it was raining.

TOO MUCH THROTTLE

During the 1948 British Grand Prix at Silverstone, the Maserati driven by Baron Emmanuel de Graffenreid spun into a potato field. It emerged with an additional attachment in the form of a commentator's microphone cable. Alas the commentator in question was unaware of this until the microphone was suddenly whipped from his grasp and he was nearly throttled by the cable.

FALL GUY

British driver Tony Fall was disqualified from the 1969 TAP Rally in Portugal for having his wife – an unauthorized passenger – in the car when it crossed the finish line.

MECHANICAL ERROR

*O*n the eve of the 1933 Mille Miglia, one of the Alfa Romeos went up in flames when an electric spark ignited petrol vapour. For some reason, nobody thought to inform the driver, Franco Cortese, of this potentially important development and he arrived four hours before the race was due to start to find that his car was little more than a burnt-out shell. However with commendable calm, Cortese refused to panic and promptly organized the rebuilding of the car. All went amazingly well until, with just an hour to go, one of the mechanics accidentally poured a can of water into the fuel tank which therefore had to be completely dismantled and cleaned. The upshot was that Cortese was considerably late for the start.

CHANGING TACK

There was more than a hint of suspicion that the host nation were up to their old tricks during motor cycling's 1904 International Cup in France. The cause of such unworthy thoughts was the sudden appearance of a cluster of nails scattered on one half of the road. The French riders somehow knew exactly which line to take to avoid getting a puncture but teams from Britain, Austria, Denmark and Germany were less fortunate. But just in case one of the Frenchman did slip up, a travelling motorcycle touring the circuit in the opposite direction kindly provided the French team with spares en route. Significantly, the other teams were not permitted this facility. I leave you to draw your own conclusions.

MONTE MAYHEM

*T*he 1973 Monte Carlo Rally was nothing less than a fiasco. Things began to go awry when a number of cars crashed on a special stage on the Burzet loop, causing a mass blockage. Consequently, no fewer than 145 cars were unable to tackle that stage – through no fault of their own. In a fit of pique, the organizers promptly disqualified them while the surviving 65 entrants pressed on towards Monaco. But the disqualified crews were not prepared to take the matter lying down and angrily set off across country to Digne where they blocked the rally route and readied themselves for a pitched battle. Some competitors, officially still in the rally, had to find alternative routes, some charged around the barricades and some simply threatened violence. The organizers' sole response was to offer the disqualified crews free entries for 1974. As it turned out, that wasn't much of a carrot to dangle – the 1974 rally was cancelled because the Middle East War had disrupted oil supplies.

WIPE-OUT

In one of the most bizarre incidents in motor racing history, a single crash at the 1927 Le Mans 24-Hour Race destroyed the chances of the entire three-car Bentley team. The prelude to this catastrophe was the spinning of a Schneider car at the White House corner. It half-blocked the road, forcing Callingham's 4-litre Bentley to roll into a ditch where it was followed moments later by Duller's 3-litre Bentley, at the time a full two laps adrift of its more powerful team-mate. Close behind, Sammy Davis in the third Bentley managed to avoid the ditch but still sustained extensive damage. It took him half an hour to get going again by which time his chance had gone. Back in the pits, the Bentley team could scarcely believe their mass misfortune.

SNOW DROP

With the 1968 Monte Carlo Rally well into its final night, among those vying for the lead was Gerard Larrousse in a works Alpine–Ranault. But his chances of victory disappeared on the treacherous mountain roads when he crashed into a huge pile of fresh snow, said to have been shovelled into the road by drunken spectators.

IRATE CROWD

The 1927 Grand Prix de Provence at Miramas was a catalogue of disasters, all of which succeeded in infuriating the spectators. The race had already been delayed for a considerable time owing to bad weather but at last the drivers were on the grid. However, they hadn't even completed the warming-up lap when a minor collision led to the immediate withdrawal of the three Talbot–Darracqs. But nobody bothered to keep the crowd informed until eventually, fed up with yet more delays and the depleted field, they rushed onto the track, thereby stopping the race, and proceeded to vandalize the Talbot team's pit equipment.

TOO YOUNG

British driver Johnny Herbert excelled himself to take fifth place with his Benetton in the 1989 United States Grand Prix at Phoenix but a local American firm reportedly refused him a hire car because he was under 25!

A VERY VERY VERY NICE MAN

*H*aving covered all but the last 150 miles of the arduous 6,000 mile La Caracas road race from Buenos Aires to Caracas in 1948, Oscar Galvez was a clear two and a half

minutes ahead of the second-placed driver and was
apparently cruising to victory. But then disaster struck and
his car broke down. Stranded in the middle of Venezuela,
Galvez looked on in despair as his two nearest rivals sped
past him before help arrived. Finally, a generous spectator in
his own car pushed Galvez bumper to bumper all the way
into Caracas so that he could finish third.

WRONG GEAR

At the 1983 German Grand Prix at Hockenheim, Niki Lauda
finished fifth in his McLaren–Ford, only to be later
disqualified for reversing in the pit lane.

CAMPARI ON THE ROCKS

Towards the end of the 1932 Mille Miglia near Ancona,
the leading car was Guiseppe Campari's Alfa Romeo.
But with victory in sight, his co-driver Sozzi crashed
into a wall. Campari was so livid at being forced out of
the race that he had to be forcibly restrained from taking
a hammer to the unfortunate Sozzi.

MISPLACED ENTHUSIASM

Immediately after the Second World War, the British
enjoyed the rare experience of popularity in France. This
enthusiasm extended to our competitors in the Monte Carlo
Rally. Indeed the civic welcome in Boulogne for British
crews frequently lasted so long that the cars were up to an
hour late leaving town. As a result, many were penalized at
the next control at Luxembourg!

SIGN OF THE TIMES

G eorge Grinton was happily leading the 1925 sidecar TT until a pit signal carrying the lone figure '3' made him think he was three minutes in front. Believing the race to be in the bag and not wishing to take any unnecessary risks, he slowed right down, only to discover he was really only three seconds ahead. By the time he had regained full power, it was too late. Two rivals had roared past him and he ended up finishing a dejected third.

TWO MINUTES TOO LATE

T here was only one real winner in the 1928 Monte Carlo Rally – and that was the weather. It certainly wasn't Donald Healey in his Triumph Super Seven. Healey had intended starting the rally from Riga but heavy snow meant that he was unable to reach the Baltic Sea port and so he had to revise his plans and start from Berlin instead. Undaunted, he braved the blizzards through Germany, Belgium and France and looked like being one of only 24 of the 93 competitors to finish within the time limit. But after trailing across Europe, he was undone so near to home at Nice where a helpful local inadvertently gave him the wrong directions. Driving as fast as the conditions would permit, Healey frantically tried to make up the lost time on the last leg to Monte Carlo, only to arrive at his destination two minutes outside the time limit.

BOXING

LEAST SUCCESSFUL BOUT

Staging the world middleweight title fight between Johnny Reagan and Jack 'Nonpareil' Dempsey on the sea front at Long Island on 13 December 1887 must have sounded like a promoter's dream. But there was one tiny problem and the fight soon had to be abandoned when the tide came in, flooding the ring. Undeterred, they found another spot several miles away and the contest resumed later that day.

SHORTEST FIGHT

Even the most inept of boxers usually manage to last ten seconds in the ring, if only so that they can be counted out. But one D. Emerson, a would-be pugilist from Pahiatura, failed to survive that long against Ross Cleverley of the Royal New Zealand Air Force in a middleweight bout at Palmerston, New Zealand, on 8 July 1952. Emerson was barely in an upright position after getting up off his stool before he was floored by the appropriately-named Cleverley. The referee took one look at the prone Emerson and immediately stopped the contest without even bothering to count.

ALL OVER IN FOUR SECONDS

Not far behind Emerson was Pat Brownson who was felled with the first punch of the fight by Mike Collins in a Golden Gloves tournament at Minneapolis on 4 November 1947. Again the referee decided not to waste anybody's time by counting and declared the contest over in just four seconds.

FATHER KNOWS BEST

The battle for the middleweight gold medal at the 1908 London Olympics was a close-fought affair between Britain's John Douglas and Australia's Reg 'Snowy' Baker. Most observers thought that Baker had shaded the verdict however and there was an element of disbelief when the decision was awarded to Douglas. Baker immediately complained that the referee was biased – an understandable sentiment in view of the fact that the referee was Douglas's father! Despite the protests of the Australian camp, Douglas kept the fight and the title.

KNOCKED HIMSELF OUT

In 1938, Irish boxer Jack Doyle was sizing up his opponent Eddie Thompson. Suddenly, Doyle saw his opening and swung a mighty punch. Alas, he missed Thompson altogether and crashed out of the ring, knocking himself out.

IN A FIX

What is believed to be the least successful attempt to fix a world championship fight took place in 1922. Battling Siki from Senegal alleged that it had been arranged that he should be knocked out in the fourth round of his light-heavyweight title contest with France's Georges Carpentier. However, Siki changed his mind when he came to the conclusion that Carpentier did not hit hard enough. Instead he went on to k.o. Carpentier in the sixth.

THE BILL AND BENN

In 1989 police mistakenly issued a photograph of boxer Nigel Benn as a wanted gunman. Two people tried to make citizen's arrests, with one actually grabbing hold of Benn and jumping on top of him. Later Benn announced that he was going to train in the United States, adding: 'I'm going to lead a monk's life.'

FIRST CHAMPIONSHIP FIGHT

Farnborough in Hampshire was the unlikely setting for what is thought to have been the first world championship contest. It took place on 17 April 1860 between Tom Sayers, the champion of England, and John C. Heenan, champion of the United States. All went well until the 37th round when the police turned up and tried to stop the fight. Soon there were far more than just the two boxers in the ring and although they managed to carry on for another five rounds, the spectacle had degenerated into one of total chaos. So the fight was stopped and declared a draw. So after all that blood and sweat, neither man achieved the honour of becoming the first world champion. That distinction was to go to London's Tom King who defeated Heenan three years later.

KNOCKED OUT REFEREE

Former German middleweight champion Pete Muller seemed to take exception to referee Max Pippow. For during the eighth round of the fight with Berlin's Hans Stretz on 7 June 1952 in Muller's home city of Cologne, Muller felled the ref with a punch, a gesture which resulted in him being barred for life by the German Boxing Association.

SUCKER PUNCH

The World Heavyweight Title fight between Primo Carnera, 'The Ambling Alp', and Max Baer on 14 June 1934 turned into a contest between Carnera's head and Baer's right hand. Eleven times Baer floored the reigning champion with that lethal weapon. Once, late in the fight, Baer feinted to throw a right and Carnera fell for it, literally, going down without a blow being landed. By then it had almost become second nature for the Italian to hit the canvas. Baer himself nearly fell over laughing but shortly afterwards, in the 11th round, the referee put Carnera out of his misery by stopping the fight.

RAPID K.O.

One of the briefest excursions into the ring was that by Ralph Walton against Al Couture at Lewiston, Maine, on 23 September 1946. Walton was still adjusting his gum shield in his corner when Couture knocked him out cold. The fight officially ended after ten and a half seconds – and that included the ten-second count!

MOST KNOCK DOWNS

Under the old Prize Ring rules, every knock-down signalled the end of a round which meant that in 1825 Patsy Tunney was felled no fewer than 276 times by Jack Jones during a fight in Cheshire. Under Queensberry Rules, this dubious distinction belongs to Christy Williams who was knocked down 41 times by one Battling Nelson in a bout at Hot Springs, Arkansas, on 26 December 1902. Having spent more time on the canvas than Van Gogh, Williams was finally knocked out for a full count in round 17.

SURPRISED WINNER

Ghana's Clement Quartey was so shocked to be declared the winner of the 1962 Empire and Commonwealth Games light-welterweight gold medal at the expense of Dick McTaggart that he fainted and had to be revived by officials.

THE VANISHING REFEREE

On 29 August 1877, John Knifton fought Tom Scrutton in London for the World Heavyweight Championship. It was an endurance bout for a purse of £25. It was a relatively uneventful affair until the ninth round when fighting broke out among the spectators. The proprietor of the venue, fearing for his property, decided to turn out the gas lights and plunged the whole place into darkness. Eventually peace was restored and the lighting returned but plans to continue the fight were scuppered when it was discovered that the referee, Mr. J. Jenn, had gone home in the confusion.

CARRIED ON FIGHTING

When 1932 Olympic heavyweight boxing champion, Argentinian Santiago Lovell, returned home after the Games, instead of receiving a hero's welcome he was sent to jail. It emerged that he had 'breached the peace' on the ship which transported the Argentinian team back from Los Angeles to Buenos Aires.

BOTH BOXERS DOWN

During a world lightweight title fight at Vernon, California, on 14 July 1912, the champion Adolph Wolgast and challenger Joe Rivers connected with simultaneous blows in the 13th round, as a result of which both dropped to the canvas. Neither appeared capable of getting to their feet until referee Jack Welch intervened. He promptly lifted Wolgast to a semi-standing position and propped him up while counting out the luckless Rivers. Presumably such were the perks that went with being the reigning champion.

LASTED THE DISTANCE

Following his middleweight gold medal at the 1968 Mexico Olympics , Chris Finnegan was selected for a random drugs test. This meant providing a sample but Finnegan was so dehydrated after the exertions of the bout that he was unable to oblige. But the authorities refused to take no for an answer and for the next few hours the men in white coats pursued him all over Mexico City in the hope of catching a few drops. Wherever Finnegan went, they went too, clutching the still empty specimen bottle. By now Finnegan was becoming a little embarrassed at his continuing failure to perform to order until at 2am, mid-way through a celebration dinner and with a bladder full of Mexican beer, he pushed his chair back from the table , beamed and announced: 'I think I'm ready to go now.' He did, and fortunately the sample was negative.

VESTED INTEREST

The consensus of opinion among those at the ringside was that James J. Corbett, soon to be World Heavyweight Champion, was definitely gaining the upper hand in his 1891 bout with Australian-based West Indian Peter Jackson. Then in the 60th round, referee Hiram Cook mysteriously exited from the ring to enter conversation with a group of gamblers who had backed Jackson. Suddenly in the next round, he stopped the fight and announced: 'No contest. All bets off.' Jackson collapsed as he left the ring so he was clearly on his last legs. Nevertheless, the result went down in the record books as a draw, albeit a highly dubious one aided by a distinctly partial referee.

FIRST CUT IS THE DEEPEST

At Leicester on 13 March 1989, Hull's Ian Bockes got up from his stool at the start of the fight and walked straight into a punch from home town boy Eugene Brown who was making his professional debut. Bockes staggered to his feet after a count of six but the referee decided he was unfit to continue and stopped the contest.

REFEREE HAD TO RETIRE

The world light-heavyweight title bout between Joey Maxim and Ray Robinson at the Yankee Stadium, New York, was a grim struggle. The fight took place during a heatwave in June 1952 and the conditions tested not only the fitness of both boxers but also that of the referee, Ruby Goldstein. In the end, it was the ref who cracked first and had to retire at the close of the tenth round out of sheer exhaustion at constantly having to pull the pair out of clinches.

STRANGE TWIST

Frenchman Rene Jacquot lost his WBC super-welterweight
title to John Mugabi of Uganda in the first round of their
1989 decider. But it was not as a result of anything that
Mugabi did – Jacquot had to retire after twisting his ankle.

THE REFEREE'S WORD WAS FINAL

The legendary Wyatt Earp acted as referee when
Cornishman Bob Fitzsimmons met Tom Sharkey at
the National Athletic Club, San Francisco, on 2
December 1896. Rumours were circulating that the
fight had been fixed so that Sharkey would win and
subsequent events certainly seemed to bear out that
theory. For Fitzsimmons was comfortably ahead in the
eighth round when Earp suddenly stopped the contest
and declared Sharkey the winner on a foul. There was
pandemonium and Fitzsimmons protested vehemently
to Earp who responded by drawing a gun and ordering
the fighter away. For some reason, that seemed to settle
the argument.

UNHAPPY DEBUT

Both Harvey Gartley and his opponent, Dennis Outlette,
were more than a shade apprehensive about what was for
both of them a first fight in public. The event was a regional
bantamweight heat of the Saginaw Golden Gloves
Championships in Michigan in 1977, and it was probably
that fear of the unknown which accounted for why after 47
seconds of the first round, neither boxer had actually
succeeded in landing a punch. Indeed, there is frequently
more brutal physical contact in the average heat of *Come*

Dancing. The spectators were beginning to grow restless and, possibly sensing this hostile atmosphere, Gartley decided to take the matter into his own hands and try to hit his opponent. He aimed an almighty blow in the vague direction of Outlette, missed by a considerable distance and promptly collapsed in a heap on the canvas. He was counted out. It is not known whether this fine man ever pursued his boxing career.

WORST-DRESSED BOXER

When Irishman John McConnell turned up to fight Charley Davis for the English Middleweight Title in London in 1873, he found that the bag containing his ring gear had gone missing. A long delay ensued while substitute garments were produced until, to the vast amusement of the crowd, he entered the ring wearing an old pair of cricketing trousers that had been made for a man at least a foot shorter and about a foot wider. If this was not handicap enough, McConnell also had no ice in his corner. As he floundered around the ring trying to hitch his trousers up, all the while sweating buckets, it was little wonder that he lost.

ONE-WAY TRAFFIC

Eddie Risko certainly knew he had been in a fight after taking on Jock McAvoy in New York on 20 December 1935. Risko was eventually knocked out just before the bell signalled the end of the first round but he had spent much of the previous three minutes on the floor. In fact, it was calculated that in just 2min 28sec of actual fighting, he was knocked down six times. The end probably came as something of a relief.

A BRIDGE TOO FAR

Bob Fitzsimmons' fight with Irishman Peter Maher in 1892 was scheduled to take place in Langtry, Texas, but when the boxers arrived, a posse of Texas Rangers were waiting to make sure that it did not go ahead. It was then that the entrepreneurial skills of Judge Roy Bean, who happened to be a friend of the promoter, came to the fore. He suggested hiring a team of men to erect a ring across the border in Mexico, reached via a pontoon bridge hastily thrown over the Rio Grande. The boxers, officials and more than 200 spectators trekked across the border and the tent was guarded by none other than Bat Masterson, Marshal of Dodge City, who stood at the entrance with six-shooters drawn to deter any possible troublemakers. After all that effort, Fitzsimmons knocked Maher out in just over a minute. And it was the only contest on the bill!

THE BITER BIT

*T*here were yet more accusations of nationalistic bias in the 1924 Paris Olympics when, in the preliminary bouts of the middleweight division, Great Britain's Harry Mallin, the defending champion, was repeatedly fouled by his French opponent. The clinches were so rough that Mallin ended the fight with teeth marks on his chest. Yet despite this, the hopelessly outclassed Frenchman was declared the winner. This was too much for the British camp to take and they instantly lodged an appeal. And with the backing of all of the English-speaking countries who threatened to withdraw if the appeal was not upheld, the decision was duly reversed and the Frenchman was thrown out.

WAYWARD PUNCH

Attempting to connect with the head of his opponent, American Mike DeCosmo, Watford welterweight Laurie Buxton missed the target but instead landed a knockout blow squarely on the chin of referee Joey Walker. Officials rushed to the dazed Walker's aid but it was some time before he was able to return to his feet. Buxton said later: 'It was a great shame – particularly since it was one of the hardest punches I'd thrown all night.' When referee Walker eventually came round, he mourned: 'I guess I can't take a punch like I used to.' With Walker too shaken to continue in control, a substitute referee took over the remainder of the ten-round contest (at Newark, New Jersey, on 18 May 1948) and to show there were no hard feelings, went on to declare Buxton the winner on points.

SWIFT DEMISE

Nigeria's Bob Roberts lasted just ten seconds of his fight with Swindon lightweight Teddy Barker at Maesteg in September 1957. Roberts was floored by the very first punch and although he got to his feet, the referee stopped it without a count. Notting Hill's Harry Deamer only managed to survive a second longer against Jack Cain in a 1922 lightweight novices' competition at London's National Sporting Club. Deamer was knocked out straight away and the contest was officially over in 11 seconds – including the count.

IN THE DEAD CORNER...

With the fight ebbing away from him, a boxer in the Philippines decided to take stern action to swing the contest back in his favour. He pulled a knife from his shorts and attacked his opponent. He was then shot dead by a policeman in the audience. It was believed his opponent was declared the winner on a technical knock-out.

CHAMP CHOMPED

Just about the least successful attempt to nobble an opponent occurred during the 1878 World Middleweight Championship bout between Ireland's Denny Harrington and American George Rooke in London. In the sixth round, there was an almighty fracas during which the referee and the timekeeper were jostled about and both fighters finished up on the floor. While Harrington was down, he was bitten on the wrist by one of Rooke's supporters, an act clearly designed to reduce his punching power. When order was restored, the Irishman showed the injury to the referee who, since he had been unsighted at the time of the savagery, ordered the fight to be continued. Within thirty seconds of the resumption, Harrington showed that he was none the worse for the experience by knocking Rooke out.

MOTHER'S PRIDE

Minna Wilson just couldn't take any more as she watched her son Tony on the receiving end of a third-round battering from Steve McCarthy in a light-heavyweight contest at Southampton in 1989. She decided that if her boy couldn't beat McCarthy, then she would. So with Tony desperately trying to fend off further blows on the ropes, Mrs Wilson clambered into the ring, removed one of her high-heeled shoes and, to the delight of the crowd, began hitting McCarthy around the head with it. The referee quickly

intervened but not before Mrs Wilson had inflicted
considerably more damage than her son on the unfortunate
McCarthy. Bleeding from a cut to the head, which he
claimed was the result of Mrs Wilson's soft-shoe shuffle,
McCarthy refused to box on, only to be disqualified for
failing to continue with the fight. Amazingly, Wilson was
declared the winner but a re-match was ordered and this
time Mrs Wilson was banned from attending.

TIME GENTLEMEN, PLEASE

An unholy row broke out between the referee and the
timekeeper in the course of a bout at Madison Square
Garden on 12 March 1948. It happened after Marcel
Cerdan, a French Moroccan, had floored Texan
Lawrence Roach with a right-hander. However as Roach
toppled, he pulled his opponent down with him. Cerdan
quickly got to his feet but then the argument began
between the two officials over their different
interpretations of the incident. Referee Arthur Donovan
reckoned it was a knockdown and wanted to start a
count, but timekeeper Jack Watson insisted that Roach
had slipped and therefore refused to count. As the war of
words continued, Roach remained on the canvas, slowly
coming to his senses. He had been there 24 seconds
before the count finally began and he got up at eight. So
the count had lasted an unbelievable 32 seconds. Not
that the rest did Roach much good – he was stopped in
the eighth round.

NO GLOVES

Surely the unluckiest disqualification in the history of
boxing was that of Sierra Leone heavyweight John Coker
before the 1966 Empire and Commonwealth Games in

Kingston, Jamaica. His crime? His hands were too big. Poor Coker, who was also an Oxford rugby blue, was unable to find a pair of gloves anywhere in Kingston that were large enough to fit his outsize hands, especially his exceptionally long thumbs. Consequently, he was disqualified prior to the competition for failing to be properly equipped.

MISCELLANEOUS MISHAPS

TOO OBLIGING

Having won the Tour de France in 1988, Spaniard Pedro Delgado was confident of retaining his title. But he could only manage third place in 1989, principally because he lost nearly three minutes at the start in Luxembourg while he was busy signing autographs!

WORST TENNIS PLAYER

As has been intimated elsewhere in this book, Luxembourg has never been renowned for its phenomenal sporting prowess. Nowhere was this truer than in the Davis Cup where for years on end, their finest tennis players met with virtually unbroken failure. The heroic stalwart of their team was one G. Wertheim who turned out for ten successive years of Davis Cup ties and only ever won one set. He announced his arrival on the world stage in 1947 when in two singles rubbers against Belgium, he won a mere seven games. For good measure, he also lost his doubles match. Monsieur Wertheim fared even worse against France two years later when in his two singles defeats, he succeeded in winning only five games. But then in 1952, the world of tennis sat back in amazement as it appeared that Wertheim had met an even worse player than himself. For in the Davis Cup tie with Egypt at Mondorf-les-Bains, he trounced M. Coen 6–0 in the second set. Clearly the shock proved too much for our hero since he quickly lost the next two sets to go down 2–6, 6–0, 2–6, 2–6. Of course, even the great tennis players cannot continue indefinitely – there comes a time when ageing legs are simply too much of a handicap. And so in 1957, Wertheim bowed out of international competition after the tie with Poland, his exit possibly hastened by a 0–6, 0–6, 0–6 defeat to A. Licis. It was good to know that he had obviously lost none of that old ability.

GOOD FOR PLANTS?

*A*rriving for an exhibition match at a club near Blackburn, snooker player Dennis Taylor was greeted enthusiastically by an official at the establishment. Bursting with pride, he said: 'You'll be OK tonight, Mr. Taylor. The table is in first-class condition and I know you're going to like it.' 'Why's that!' inquired Taylor. 'Because I washed it for you specially this afternoon.' 'And he wasn't joking,' says Taylor. 'The cloth was absolutely saturated.'

THE EAGLE HAS LANDED

In recent years one man has become synonymous with the spirit of the Great British Loser. I speak, of course, of Eddie 'The Eagle' Edwards, ski jumper extraordinary. Having made last place his own in a number of events, 'The Eagle' soared in a 1989 World Cup event at Lake Placid when he finished ahead of the Dutchman Gerrit Konijnenberg on 'style'.

Taking into account non-finishers, Edwards' final placing was a remarkable 78th out of 83, causing him to remark, in the manner of season professionals: 'I kicked some butt.' Talking about this sudden improvement, he added: 'I'm going down thinking about my position, making contact, exploding on take-off, keeping my head down, getting into a good flight position. All of that is going through my mind, instead of just "Ooooh."' But it was a comfort to know that he wasn't lost to us forever. A week later he broke his collarbone in practice, admitting: 'The jump was so good and I was in such a good flight position that I started to panic.'

SCUPPERED

*P*eterborough *Pirates ice hockey team lost 26 games in a row in the Heineken League Premier Division during season 1985–86. A club spokesman said: 'We are looking for an improvement next season.'*

GREYHOUND BRAWL

The 1931 Greyhound Derby ended in chaos after one dog, Ryland R, had been found guilty of fighting. Coming round the final bend, Ryland R had 'interfered' with Seldom Led, causing the latter to finish last. Ryland R was duly disqualified and the race declared void, much to the disgust of the supporters of Mick the Miller who had been the first dog past the post, thereby completing a hat-trick of Greyhound Derbys. But the officials were adamant and a re-run was ordered from which Ryland R was banned. However, the rest between the two races was too short for five-year-old Mick the Miller and he could only trail in fourth at the second attempt.

BIG MOUTH

American tennis player Gardnar Mulloy had suggested, apparently in jest, that the draws for Wimbledon were fixed. But the committee did not take kindly to such remarks, however flippant. So for the 1949 championships, he was invited to pull the names out of the hat himself. He was out of luck since he pulled his own name out last – drawn against the No. 1 seed Ted Schroeder. So Mulloy went out in the first round and Schroeder (who was incidentally his doubles partner) went on to win the singles title.

MISSED HIS CUE

Mike Watterson was due to meet Bob Harris in a qualifying round match of the 1982 Coral UK Snooker Championships at Sheffield Snooker Centre. As promoter of the event as well as proprietor of the venue, one would have expected

Watterson to have been perfectly prepared for the contest. However, he was late for the start of the match and had to forfeit one frame.

DUTCH DEBACLE

*H*ugolein van Hoorn must have wondered whether it was worth making the trip from her native Netherlands to compete in the 1988 British Under-21 Open Squash Championships at Lamb's Squash Club in London. Up against Britain's Lucy Souter, the Dutch girl lost 0–9, 0–9, 0–9 in just seven and a half minutes.

UNDERWATER MAYHEM

One thing with water polo is that you don't get many pitch invasions. But there are sometimes flare-ups between rival players although few as serious as that which took place in the semi-final at the 1956 Melbourne Olympics. It was not so much the fact that both teams were just one step away from the final which caused the tension, it was more a question of the political situation at the time. For the competing countries were Hungary and the Soviet Union. The Swedish referee did his best to keep control but as the niggling increased, he decided to abandon the game because, in his opinion, it had degenerated into a 'boxing match under water'. Hungary were leading 4–0 at the time and went on to win the gold with the Russians getting the bronze.

PHLEGMATIC

*A*n ice hockey game without a mass brawl is like a soccer match without a kick-off. Tempers ran particularly high in a clash between Montreal Canadians and Buffalo Sabres, so much so that Canadians' Denis Savard spat at an opposing player. Unfortunately, his spitting was no more accurate than his passing that night and he missed his intended target and hit one of the match officials instead. The official remained commendably cool but Savard was sent off, giving him time to clear his head as well as his throat.

TOO COLD FOR HUSKY RACING

Britain's first husky sled championships, scheduled for 28 February 1993, were called off because it was too cold for the dogs. An organizer of the event, in the Kielder Forest, Northumbria, said: 'We've had temperatures of minus nine degrees Centigrade. The ice and snow have made it far too dangerous.'

MORE PRACTICE NEEDED

The African nations may be emerging forces in many sports but Swaziland clearly weren't quite ready to take centre stage at the 1980 World Bowls Championships in Melbourne. In one match they crashed 63–1 to Japan.

ALARMED

During the 1981 World Snooker Team Cup, referee John Smyth popped out one morning to buy a new battery for his portable alarm clock. He put the clock in his jacket pocket and forgot all about it. But in the afternoon it went off mid-way through a match between John Spencer and Paddy Morgan. Proceedings were halted while Smyth rummaged around to find the off button.

HIS BOTTLE WENT

Beals Wright, the United States number one, was ruled out of the 1906 Davis Cup by a bizarre sequence of events. On the eve of the American team's departure, he made a conscious decision to get drunk, knowing that he had the long sea voyage to England on which to recover before he was again required to wield a racket in earnest. Waking up in the team hotel the following morning, he experienced that familiar sensation of a dry mouth and rang for a bottle of soda water. It arrived unopened and Wright was without a bottle opener. Instead of ringing down for one, he unaccountably attempted to open it with a toothbrush (whether he was also in the practice of cleaning his teeth with a corkscrew we do not know). The exercise was doomed to failure and the neck of the bottle smashed in his right hand. Bleeding profusely, he called out for help before fainting. Sadly, the wound became infected and Wright developed blood poisoning. Indeed, one finger had to be amputated. Needless to say, he was forced to withdraw from the Davis Cup, all because he had fancied a few drinks.

TAKING DEFEAT TO HEART

It could be argued that Myiesha Bradford of Richmond, California, over-reacted just a little when she allegedly shot and paralysed her husband Alvin in 1989 because she was angry that he had rolled a gutter ball, thereby losing a ten-pin bowling match.

FOXES ON THE RUN

The motto of Friendsville Academy Foxes basketball team was 'Humble in victory, praiseworthy in defeat'. They must have dispensed a great deal of praise between 1967 and 1973 when they managed to lose 128 successive games. The small-town American team only had one cheerleader and their tactical know-how was, to put it mildly, limited. Their coach admitted: 'I used to give them pep talks until I realized it was making them nervous.' An indication of their prowess can be gauged from the fact that a gentleman by the name of Phil Patterson was voted the club's player of the year for 1970 even though he hadn't scored a single point all season.

HOCKEY HUMILIATIONS

In a ladies' hockey international at Merton, South London, on 3 February 1923, France went down 23–0 to England. The men of India went one better during the 1932 Los Angeles Olympics when they thrashed the United States 24–1...a result which didn't go down too well with the home crowd.

FINAL FLIGHT

A racing pigeon owned by the first Duke of Wellington was released from a sailing ship off the Ichabo Islands, West Africa, on 8 April 1845. Across continents it flew, defying storms and scorching sun, until on 1 June, 55 days and at least 5,400 miles later and just a mile from its loft at Nine Elms, Wandsworth, it dropped dead.

WASHED OUT

Rarely has an event been more chaotic than the 1955 US National Men's Doubles tennis tournament. It was scheduled to take place between Monday 15 August and Sunday 21 August 1955 and for the first two days, everything

ran comparatively smoothly. Then hurricane 'Diane' hit town and three days of torrential rain left the grass courts at Longwood Cricket Club, Boston, looking like paddy fields. At one stage, the water level was higher than the net posts. By the Saturday, the day before the tournament was due to end, the first round hadn't even been completed. Then as yet more rain started to fall, players began to drop out. The list of withdrawals was lengthened by the forthcoming Davis Cup final between the United States and Australia which was due to begin the following Friday. Seeing no end in sight at Boston, both team captains immediately ordered their players to scratch from the National Doubles. In total, 14 pairs withdrew, including five from the third round and two from the quarter-finals. One duo even dropped out at match point. And because the courts were so damp, the matches tended to be long, drawn-out affairs. It was an organizer's nightmare. What remained of the tournament finally reached a conclusion a week late, the winners being an unseeded pair from Japan.

CAUGHT HARE

*A*t the very first greyhound meeting at Wembley on 10 December 1927, a dog called Palatinus caught the hare before the race had finished. There had to be a re-run.

WORST NETMINDER

Richard Copland, netminder for Irvine Magnum Wings ice hockey team, made quite an impact in the 1986–87 season. He only played in two matches for the Scottish club, in the course of one weekend in November, but let in a total of 56 goals – 24 against Peterborough Pirates and 32 against Lee Valley Lions. In fact he faced just 122 shots in all, nearly half of which ended up in the back of his net. His record of conceding a goal almost every two minutes has unfortunately proved a tough act to follow.

LOWE BLOW

The hushed tones of that doyen of snooker commentators, Ted Lowe, were heard to splendid effect in a match involving Fred Davis. Faced with an awkward shot, Davis attempted to straddle the corner of the table but found the position uncomfortable and therefore switched the cue to his left hand. At which Ted informed the watching millions: 'Fred Davis is 67 years of age now and he's obviously a little too old to get his leg over.' Realizing what he had said, Ted tried to qualify his statement: 'As you can see, he prefers to use his left hand instead.'

WASTE OF ENERGY

*T*he final of the light-heavyweight wrestling at the 1912
Stockholm Olympics was a close-fought contest. In fact it
was so close that it was impossible to separate Anders
Ahlgren of Sweden and Ivar Bohling from Finland...even
after nine hours of wrestling. At that point, the judges
decided they'd seen enough and stopped the bout, giving
both men silver medals. No gold was awarded. All that
effort for nothing...

A RIGHT SHOWER

T he Toronto Blue Jays baseball team couldn't wait to
show off their new stadium for 1989, the Skydome,
the first in the country with a retractable roof. But at
the opening ceremony they were caught out by a sudden
downpour. None of the spectators had brought
umbrellas and it took 34 minutes to put the wonder roof
up, by which time everyone was soaked to the skin.

GAME, SET AND MATCH

B arely had she taken her tennis racket out of her bag than a
Miss C. Wolf was putting it back again, ready to go home.
For she had been beaten 0–6, 0–6 by Pauline Betz in the 1943
Tri-State Tournament at Pennsylvania. And she hadn't won a
single point. A similar humiliation had befallen a Miss
Huiskamp in Seattle 33 years earlier. She had battled through
her encounter with Hazel Hotchkiss, also without winning a
point. At least British dental student J. Sandiford managed to
extract one point from his match with Australia's J.E. Harper
in the 1946 Sutton Tournament. But that was all, as
Sandiford fell 0–6, 0–6 in just 18 minutes.

NO SMOKE WITHOUT FIRE

*T*he 1980 Davis Cup final between Czechoslovakia and
Italy in Prague was a fiery confrontation. The Italian
supporters were at their most excitable as they loudly
queried what they considered to be unfair umpiring
decisions. The situation boiled over in the fifth set of the
match between Tomas Smid and Adriano Panatta. The score
stood at 3–3 when play was held up for 45 minutes following
the arrest of an Italian spectator. According to the Czech
police, the offender (who it later transpired was a lawyer and
the brother of a prominent Communist politician in Italy)
was ejected from the hall for violating a no-smoking rule.
His friends denied the charge and insisted that he had
merely been cheering 'in a normal manner'. The Italian team
flatly refused to play on until the man was allowed to return
to his seat. Ironically it was Italy's Panatta whose
concentration was wrecked by the interruption. He went on
to lose the match and the Czechs took the Cup.

THE PRICE OF FAME

Having won the men's figure skating title in 1920, 1924 and
1928, Sweden's Gillis Grafstrom had high hopes of
completing a four-timer at the 1932 Winter Olympics at Lake
Placid. As a result of his achievements, Grafstrom was quite
a celebrity at the Games and a movie camera was on hand to
record his exploits. Alas, the camera literally proved
Grafstrom's downfall during the compulsory figures. For it
was allowed too near and part-way through his routine,
Grafstrom collided with it, falling heavily and suffering mild
concussion. Consequently, the hapless Swede had to settle
for the silver medal behind Austrian Karl Schafer.

FAST FRAME

*P*oor Patsy Fagan found that Alex Higgins lived up to his
'Hurricane' nickname in a frame at the Irish Professional
Snooker Championships. Higgins raced to a break of 122 and
won the frame in just 2min 45sec. One wag said it would
have been even quicker if Higgins hadn't gone for a pint half-
way through!

MINE'S A DOUBLE

A bitter battle of the sexes erupted in Cornwall over
publicans' claims that women darts players were taking
too long to finish their matches. Originally, the ladies used to
have just game of 601 per match but then they insisted on
playing three like the men – and that's where the trouble
started for the Lostwithiel Darts League. Jonathan Cock, the
League secretary, said: 'The problem is they are just not good

enough to get a double to finish games. So they go on and on. I've been getting a lot of flak from landlords about ladies' matches taking so long. There will just have to be a change in the rules to try to shorten games. The men start their matches at 8pm and are finished 90 minutes later – even a bad men's match will take no longer than a couple of hours.' One landlord, who did not wish to be named, moaned: 'It's past a joke. At one match the women were still throwing at nearly 1am when the pub had closed and the staff had been sent home.'

NODDED OFF

Facing match point in his 1964 Wimbledon men's singles first round clash with South Africa's Abe Segal, American Clark Graebner hit a ball which clearly landed beyond the baseline. He waited for the inevitable call of 'out' which would signal the end of his participation in that year's competition. But none came. All eyes turned on the lineswoman, Dorothy Cavis Brown, and the reason for the silence became apparent – she had dozed off. A ball boy ran over to rouse the embarrassed official but her plight had been captured by sufficient photographers to ensure that she swiftly made world-wide headlines. She was subsequently suspended from duty and soon afterwards gave up umpiring.

MEADOWLARK YEMEN

The Yemen basketball team which took part in the 1982 Asian Games were no great threat to the Harlem Globetrotters. Their finest moment came in the match with Iraq at New Delhi. They lost by 251 points to 33.

PUTTING ON WEIGHT

F eeling confident during the weightlifting event at the
1966 Empire and Commonwealth Games, English
middleweight Louis Martin asked for a weight increase in
pounds. Alas, the officials thought he meant kilograms and he
nearly ruptured himself attempting the subsequent lift.

IN A FIX

I n 1945 the basketball team from Akron University
travelled several hundred miles across the United
States to play Brooklyn College in Boston. They arrived
to find the game had been cancelled after members of
the Brooklyn team were arrested on suspicion of fixing
matches and accepting money from professional gamblers.

SLIPPERY CUSTOMER

*T he organizers of the 1956 Winter Olympics at Cortina
D'Ampezzo in Italy must have thought they had made a
safe choice by asking Italian speed skater Guido Caroli to be
the last runner in the ceremonial relay for carrying the
Olympic torch. However, as he completed a circuit of the
arena, Caroli slipped and fell in an undignified heap. The
crowd gasped but fortunately the flame didn't go out and the
Olympic tradition remained intact.*

SNOOKER STOPPED BY RAIN

I t's not often that rain stops play in snooker but it happened
during the 1973 World Championships at the City Hall,
Manchester. Water seeped through the roof and onto the

"I THOUGHT THIS WAS MEANT TO BE SNOOKER, NOT POOL!"

table during the quarter-final between Fred Davis and Alex Higgins and play was halted while workmen carried out running repairs.

SEAT OF LEARNING

I am aware of a number of quaint pastimes that are performed in rural areas of Britain but the following item which appeared in 'Where and When in East Anglia' is, I believe, a first: 'Men's and Ladies' Singles, Pairs and Triples as well as Mixed Pairs are invited to the Yarmouth Bowling Green to compete for £5,000 of prize money at the Great Yarmouth Open Bowels Festival.'

FLYERS' WINGS CLIPPED

One of the biggest drubbings in ice hockey's Heineken League was the 41–2 by which Richmond Flyers crashed to Cleveland Bombers on 19 February 1983. But four years later, even that show of incompetence was surpassed by Telford Tornadoes who lost their Second Division match with Bristol Phantoms 49–3. A Telford official said: 'We were flattered by the scoreline.'

PLAYING IT COOL

The least enthusiastic demonstration of paternal pride in an offspring's sporting achievement was undoubtedly that of the father of tennis player Charlotte Sterry. After winning the Wimbledon ladies' singles for 1895, Miss Sterry cycled home to Surbiton, with her racket in a clip on the front fork. There she found her father clipping the hedge. 'Where have you been, dear?' he asked. 'To Wimbledon, of course, father,' she replied. 'Ah yes, I remember – you were playing the final, weren't you? Did you win?'

THE PRIDE OF THE PENTATHLON

The Tunisian team set new standards for the equestrian event in the Olympic modern pentathlon when they failed to score a single point in the 1960 Games at Rome. This was largely due to the fact that at some stage or another, the entire team fell off their horses. Nor did Tunisia exactly excel in the remainder of the pentathlon. One of their swimmers came perilously close to drowning and they were ordered from the shooting range because of fears that they were endangering the lives of the judges. When it came to the fencing, they were severely handicapped by only having one man who could fence. Behind his mask, the Tunisians hoped that nobody would realize they were sending out the same man over and over again. But in the course of this plucky little competitor's third contest, his opponent recognized him as the man he had just fought and had him disqualified. Tunisia came last.

IMPERSONATING A LINE JUDGE

Two of the leading lights in ladies tennis, Suzanne Lenglen and Helen Wills, met in a special challenge match at the Carlton Hotel, Cannes, in 1926. Naturally enough when the players heard the umpire, Commander George Hillyard, call 'Game, set and match to Mademoiselle Lenglen', they assumed it was all over. But with the ladies half-way to the dressing-room, the Commander had to summon them back because he discovered that Miss Wills' final shot had been called 'out' by someone in the crowd and not by the linesman, Lord Charles Hope, who indeed affirmed that the ball was most certainly in.

RIPPING YARN

Any snooker shot that required even a modicum of athleticism was always a problem for big Bill Werbeniuk. Once, playing Dennis Taylor in a Champion of Champions tournament, Werbeniuk bent over to line up an awkward shot when a vast rendering sound ripped across the hall. The Canadian had split his trousers. Werbeniuk muttered something (which, fortunately for those of a nervous disposition, was inaudible) and rushed out of the hall. Taylor was worried in case he could see the pink since Werbeniuk

never wore any underpants. After lengthy adjustments, Werbeniuk returned to a wall of applause normally reserved for the World Champion or Jimmy White.

NONE TOO FRIENDLY

In the so-called 'Friendly Army Tournament' at Miskolc, Hungary, in August 1981, the USSR over-ran Afghanistan 86–2 at handball.

SOMETHING TO SHOUT ABOUT

In 1989 a 12-year-old cheerleader, Angelina Perez, reportedly gave birth to a son during the third quarter of an American Football game in Guyaco, Peru. Apparently her persistent jumping up and down and general enthusiasm for the proceedings caused her to go into premature labour. It is not known whether her fellow cheerleaders responded with cries of 'Give us a B, give us an A...'

SERVED UNDERARM

When Spain entertained Brazil in Barcelona in the second round of the 1966 Davis Cup, there were hopes of an epic singles encounter between the host nation's Manuel Santana and Thomas Koch. The first set lived up to the billing with Koch edging home 7–5 but then Santana injured his shoulder and was forced to serve underarm for the rest of the match. Not surprisingly the Spaniard was unable to inject much power or guile into an underarm serve and Koch attacked him with relish. Poor Santana lost the next two sets 1–6, 1–6, and with it the match.

REDDY TEDDY GO

A teenager threw the Northern Puppy Derby at Sunderland Greyhound Stadium into turmoil one year by lobbing a teddy bear onto the track in front of the onrushing dogs . To the disgust of punters, the dogs immediately decided that the teddy looked more appetizing than the hare and set about tearing it to pieces. Inevitably the race was declared void. At court the youth, who needed a police escort from the track to avoid retribution from the irate crowd, was fined £100. He also had his teddy confiscated.

WRONG-WAY RIEGELS

The finest moment in the history of American Football occurred in the 1929 Rosebowl when 'Wrong-Way Riegels' became an overnight celebrity. California centre Roy Riegels picked up a Georgia Tech fumble on the Tech's 20-yard line and raced down the pitch – but sadly in the wrong direction towards his own goal. As the other players looked on in stunned silence, his team-mate Benny Lom rushed over to tackle Riegels on his own one-yard line. Roy's run had brought the 53,000 spectators to their feet but it proved a costly aberration. For the move resulted in Georgia scoring two vital points which enabled them to win 8–7. Riegels said later: 'I thought the noise was the fans yelling encouragement.' Yet far from being pilloried, Riegels became an unlikely all-American hero. He received a stack of fan mail including a proposal of marriage in which he and his bride would walk up the aisle instead of down!

BREAK POINT

Tennis player Lighton Ndefwayl blamed his defeat in a Zambian professional tournament on the fact that his opponent kept breaking wind. 'It made me lose my famous concentration,' complained Ndefwayl. He also moaned that his jockstrap was too tight.

AND FINALLY...

After beating 1,000 rivals in a gruelling 500-mile race, Percy the racing pigeon flopped down exhausted in his Sheffield loft...and was promptly eaten by the neighbourhood cat. To add insult to injury, the 90-minute delay in finding his remains and handing his identification tag to the judges relegated Percy from first to third place. A truly great sporting failure.